GW00697132

# Be My Guest

# Be My Guest

## Fay Lewis

Photography by Neil Corder

Décor styling by Wally Clack of Gideon's Flowers & Functions

## Dedication

*Be My Guest* is dedicated to Linda de Villiers (Publisher, Struik Lifestyle, Random House Struik) in celebration and appreciation of her commitment and contribution to the world of publishing in South Africa for over 25 years. I respect Linda's exceptional qualities of leadership, her unassuming and just approach to her responsibilities and her long service to the industry. I am proud to call her a role model and friend.

## Acknowledgements

To say this work is the result of a team effort would be an understatement. It is the product of a true collaboration between esteemed colleagues and dear friends.

I record my thanks to Cecilia Barfield for your precise editing of the manuscript and your even-keeled guidance throughout the project. Thanks also to Joy Clack for your eagle-eyed proofreading and thorough indexing.

My sincerest gratitude to Helen Henn for the elegant and striking design and for involving yourself with the whole look of the book. Thanks too for your conscientious input at so many of the photographic shoots. I so appreciate you involving me along every step of the design process.

Neil Corder, a true gem for your superlative photography, tireless efforts, and for bringing Helen's vision and my food to life. Thanks for looking at each photograph in a uniquely creative fashion. I truly appreciate the personal sacrifices you made for the sake of the book.

Wally Clack of Gideon's Flowers & Functions, for your imagination and style in creating these spectacular table settings. Thanks for your friendship and loyalty and for the heart-warming experience of creating a book with you.

Justine Kiggen, for your friendship, sensitivity, and intuition and for conscientiously attending to every detail in such a loving and professional manner. It is always a privilege to work with you.

Lisa Clark, for being the link between myself and Neil. Your understanding of composition and food fashion was invaluable during the shoots.

Katherine Freemantle, for helping in a million different ways and for making everyone smile.

Emma Wilson, for preparing the food with such loving care, calmness and attention to detail.

Jessica de Bruin, Paul Shiakallis (digital photographic assistants) and, in particular, Bernard Bronn for assisting Neil in such a professional manner and for being such an integral part of our food and design team.

I wish to thank Naomie Blom for everything and more. Shereen Fihrer for the sourcing and loan of an extensive range of local and imported goods. Eric and Rona Ellerine, Martin Ellert, Ita Stern and Elize and Dons Volschenk for all their assistance and support.

The author and publishers also wish to thank the following persons and companies for their kind assistance and/or loan of props for the photography:
The management and staff of Head Interiors; Lauren Abelheim of Apsley House for the generous loan and transportation of numerous goods; Karen Short and Wendy Tayler of Hazeldene Hall, Parktown; the directors and staff of Lejwe La Metsi Game Farm, Bela Bela; Lisa Clark and her husband Anthony Dyason; Gideon du Plessis, Pieter and Dalene van Niekerk, Richard Segerman, Corné Köhler, Anton van Zyl, Elias Teffo and staff of Gideon's Flowers & Functions.
Cover photography shot at Morrells Boutique Venue, Northcliff, Johannesburg. Sincere thanks to Bernice Morrell and Sabine Seeger.

Published in 2009 by Struik Lifestyle
(an imprint of Random House Struik (Pty) Ltd)
Company Reg. No. 1966/003153/07
80 McKenzie Street, Cape Town 8001
PO Box 1144, Cape Town, 8000, South Africa

**Publisher:** Linda de Villiers

**Editor:** Cecilia Barfield

**Designer:** Helen Henn

**Photographer:** Neil Corder

**Photographic assistant:** Bernard Bronn

**Décor stylist:** Wally Clack of Gideon's Flowers and Functions

**Project co-ordinator:** Justine Kiggen

**Food stylist:** Lisa Clark

**Food stylist's assistant:** Katherine Freemantle

**Food preparation:** Emma Wilson

**Proofreader and indexer:** Joy Clack

Copyright © in published edition:
Random House Struik (Pty) Ltd 2009
Copyright © in text: Fay Lewis 2009
Copyright © in photographs: Fay Lewis 2009

All rights reserved. No part of this publication may be reproduced,
stored in a retrieval system or transmitted, in any form or by any means,
electronic, mechanical, photocopying, recording or otherwise, without
the prior written permission of the publishers
and the copyright holders.

Reproduction: Hirt & Carter Cape (Pty) Ltd
Printing and binding: Tien Wah Press (Pte) Ltd, Singapore

ISBN 978-1-77007-780-5

Over 40 000 unique African images available to purchase from our image
bank at www.imagesofafrica.co.za

# Contents

# Introduction

My love of entertaining started in my teens when my family or friends gathered to enjoy good food, as well as one another's company. I am delighted that trends are swinging back to those days, and that there is a return to home entertaining. The word 'entertaining' is often associated with hard work and stress, but the table settings and recipes in this book will fill you with so much creativity, reflecting who you are and making every occasion a memorable one!

I have grouped the ideas and recipes into themes, but these are by no means prescriptive – shuffle them as you like to suit your personal style. I hope you will be inspired to have people over more often.

# A guide to entertaining

- Set a **date** for the party – including the day of the week and the time of day.
- Decide on the **style** of the party – formal vs. informal.
- The secret to successful entertaining is in the **planning** – start at least a week in advance and compile the menu and shopping lists.
- Plan the **main course** first. If you start off light, with a salad or a soup, build up to a crescendo with an indulgent, rich dessert!
- Compile the **task list** in chronological order and divide the shopping list into categories, i.e. butcher, grocer and fruiterer.
- Entertaining is about what **you feel like** cooking and not about what tradition dictates.
- Keep things **simple** so that ingredients taste of what they are.
- When planning the menu, consider the **age and gender** of the guests. Most children, the elderly and women tend to have smaller appetites than teenagers and men.
- Use **seasonal ingredients** and link the food to the climatic conditions.
- Take **textures and colours** into account; make sure the **flavours** are complementary.
- **Dietary requirements, food allergies** and particular **dislikes** of guests should be taken into account.
- **Combine** a variety of **cooking methods** and avoid too many fried foods.
- Ensure the number of guests suit the **location and climatic conditions**.
- **Group guests** with compatible, as well as conflicting interests, or whatever you think will work best to stimulate conversation.
- Ensure that the food and **ambience** suit the guests – formal vs. informal.
- The first 15 minutes of the party are the most important – **offer drinks immediately**.
- Make the guests **feel at home** and allow your own imperfections to show!
- **Don't disappear** for long periods of time – a well-planned menu demands no more than 15 minutes of last-minute preparation.
- **Music** establishes and sustains an easy mood – keep the volume low at the start and adjust according to the tone of the party.
- For evening parties, use a combination of **lighting and candlelight**. Use unscented candles as part of the table setting and scented candles elsewhere.
- For more formal events use **name cards** at each place setting. Create something eye-catching and unusual.
- Store the prepared food in the fridge in the **order of serving** – this saves time when serving, and ensures that nothing is left behind.
- Check the menu so that everything is **ready for serving** with all the utensils at hand.
- The **seating arrangements** should suit the style of the party. At a formal party, place the host at the top of the table and the female guest of honour to the right of the male host. The male guest of honour should be seated to the right of the hostess. Avoid seating couples together; alternate men and women.
- **Pace** the meal and don't clear the table until everyone has finished eating.
- Serve coffee in the living room to create a different ambience and allow the guests to **relax away** from the dining table.
- **Assess** the event afterwards and be honest with yourself about where you went wrong.
- Keep a **guest book** and a record of what you served to whom so as to avoid giving the same guests the same menu when next you entertain.
- REMEMBER: GOOD COMPANY + GOOD FOOD + A GOOD SETTING + GOOD PLANNING = A GREAT TIME!

## Serving styles

There are many different ways to serve a meal – those most commonly used for entertaining are:

**PLATE OR RESTAURANT STYLE** (see left): The food is plated individually in the kitchen and works best for a small party and where the kitchen is positioned close to the dining table.

**BUFFET STYLE** (see above): Guests serve themselves from one or more food stations with easy access on all sides.

**FAMILY STYLE** (see opposite page): Platters and bowls of food are passed around at the table. If the table is too small, a side table or ledge can be used as a sideboard.

Consider combining different serving styles – plating the starter and dessert, and serving the main course buffet style.

Formal place setting 1

Dessert spoon & fork

Red wine glass • White wine glass • Water glass

Bread knife

Fish fork • Meat fork

Meat knife • Fish knife • Soup spoon

Formal place setting 2

Red wine glass • Water glass • White wine glass

Bread knife

Fish fork • Meat fork • Dessert fork

Dessert spoon • Meat knife • Fish knife • Soup spoon

Informal place setting

Dessert spoon & fork

Water glass

Bread knife

Salad fork • Meat fork

Meat knife

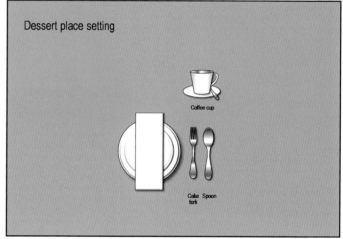

Dessert place setting

Coffee cup

Cake fork • Spoon

# Table settings and decorative elements

- Select and iron the linens you plan to use, a day in advance.
- A table is an empty space, therefore it is important to have a focal point such as a candelabra or a flower arrangement as a centrepiece.
- Set the table at least six hours before the guests arrive. It is the crockery, glassware, flowers, candles and linen with which you dress the table that makes the occasion special.
- One of the easiest ways to change the appearance of a table is to combine linens with different textures. For formal meals, use a matching cloth and napkins, and for a more casual look, combine different colours.
- Buying one new piece of crockery can completely transform the table. Be creative with your choice of colours, textures and shapes.
- Clear glasses go well with any setting, but it is also fun to introduce some coloured glasses. And of course there is nothing quite like crystal to add that extra sparkle!

## Glassware

Selecting glassware is a matter of personal taste and the thinner the glass, the better the quality. Ensure that all glassware has a cut and polished lip.

**WHITE WINE:** A stemmed, tulip-shaped glass with a tapered top.

**TUMBLER:** A short glass with no stem.

**PORT OR DESSERT WINE:** A short-stemmed, tulip-shaped glass.

**CHAMPAGNE FLUTE:** A tall, tapered glass that traps the bubbles in the champagne or sparkling wine.

**ALL-PURPOSE WINE:** A short-stemmed, longish tulip-shaped glass.

**BRANDY OR COGNAC:** A short-stemmed, tulip-shaped glass with a deep, round bowl.

**HIGHBALL:** A tall glass with straight sides.

**RED WINE:** A stemmed, tulip-shaped glass with a tapered top and a larger bowl than a white wine glass.

**LIQUEUR:** A small, short-stemmed, tulip-shaped glass smaller than a port glass.

**MARTINI:** A shorter-stemmed glass with a larger V-shaped bowl than a cocktail glass.

## Dinnerware

Good quality dinnerware with a simple design can work for any occasion. You can also mix in an antique or colourful piece to suit individual styles. White china is always a safe bet and won't upstage the food being served. Chargers or underplates are also popular and serve as a base under the first course plate; these should be removed when the main course is served.

## Cutlery

Good quality cutlery with a simple, timeless design works best for any occasion. Stainless-steel cutlery is a good choice for most meals, while sterling silver or silver-plated (e.g. EPNS) cutlery may be reserved for special occasions.

## Servingware and utensils

White platters and bowls, and silver or stainless-steel utensils will match any dinnerware. It is a good idea to add some coloured and patterned pieces to create interest. You can never have sufficient large spoons, serving forks, spatulas, and lifters at hand for serving.

## Pairing wine with food

Selecting wines that will work best with food is a matter of personal taste and there is only one rule when it comes to food and wine pairing: pair those *you* like the most! Wine and food complement each other best when their qualities are the same or in contrast. In the same way that fresh lemon is squeezed onto oysters or Parmesan is grated over pasta to combine flavours, so too the pairing of the food and wine creates different flavours, textures and aromas. Always serve wines from light to heavy as the meal progresses; serve whites before reds, and dry wines before sweet wines. Sauces on food also affect the wines: a grilled breast of chicken will match well with a light-bodied white wine such as a Chenin Blanc, but if you add a rich sauce, serve a medium- to full-bodied white wine such as a Chardonnay.

When selecting the wine (or wines) to complement a meal, take the following into account:

The **body** – is it light or heavy?
The **flavour** – what does it taste of, citrus, berry or apple?
The **character** – is it dry or fruity, what is the level of acidity?
The **intensity** – is it bold or delicate?

| TYPE OF FOOD | WINE MATCH |
|---|---|
| Appetizers and salty snack foods | Sparkling wines and Champagne |
| Spicy or smoked foods | Fruity wines – Riesling, Gewürztraminer, Chenin Blanc |
| Rich or fatty foods | Full-bodied wines – Chardonnay, Merlot, Cabernet Sauvignon |
| Acidic foods | High-acid white wines – Sauvignon Blanc |
| Fish and shellfish | Dry to off-dry whites – Chardonnay, Sauvignon Blanc, Chenin Blanc, Rosé |
| Lamb | Medium-bodied reds – Merlot, Pinot Noir, Pinotage |
| Beef | Full-bodied reds – Cabernet Sauvignon, Bordeaux Blends, Shiraz |
| Desserts | Sweet wines – Noble Late Harvest, Muscat, Port |
| Goat's-milk cheeses | High-acid white wines – Sauvignon Blanc |
| Cream cheeses | Fruity or sweet red wines – Noble Late Harvest, Young Pinot Noir, Tawny Port |
| Soft-ripened cheeses such as Brie or Camembert | Full-bodied wines – Cabernet Sauvignon, Bordeaux Blends |
| Blue cheeses | Sweet wines – Noble Late Harvest, Port, Sherry |
| Sharp, salty cheeses such as Cheddar or Parmesan | Spicy, full-bodied wines – Cabernet Sauvignon, Shiraz |

# Serving wine

- When serving a different wine with each course, allow one glass of wine per person. A 750-ml bottle of wine contains approximately five glasses. If one type of wine is served throughout, allow half a bottle per person, but keep a few extra bottles on hand!
- Serve sparkling wines well chilled at 6–7 °C and white wines at 7–10 °C. Reds and dessert wines should be served at a cool room temperature.
- Table settings should include a glass for each wine you are serving.
- Ensure the glasses are washed and dried with a CLEAN, lint-free cloth; often a glass will develop a bad odour from the detergent or drying cloth, or have bits of fluff on its surface.
- Open red wines an hour before serving and decant into a carafe or decanter. This will mellow a young wine and also add a decorative element to the table setting.
- Pour the wine once the guests are seated, and fill glasses between one-third and one-half full. This makes provision for swirling and allows the wine to breathe.
- When serving sparkling wine, first pour a small amount down the side of the glass, allowing the bubbles to settle before filling the glass three-quarters full.
- Pour white or red wine into the centre of the glass and lightly twist the bottle so that the last drop falls into the glass.

# Brunch

Warm fruit salad

Onion, ricotta and sage omelette

Smoked haddock quiche

Sweetcorn blini with crème fraîche
and salmon caviar

Roast beef with blue cheese and green peppercorn topping

Polenta flatbread

Chocolate-filled French toast

Berry fruit sorbet

# Warm fruit salad

150 g dried apricots

250 g pitted prunes

3 fresh pears, cored and cut into wedges

250 ml verjuice

grated rind of 2 oranges

250 ml freshly squeezed orange juice

30 ml freshly squeezed lemon juice

30 ml honey

mascarpone cheese, for serving

25 g hazelnuts, chopped, for serving

Preheat the oven to 180 °C. Coat an ovenproof casserole dish with cooking spray and set aside.

Combine all the ingredients, except the mascarpone and hazelnuts, in a mixing bowl, then spoon into the prepared dish. Cover with foil and bake for 50–60 minutes, or until the pears are soft. Serve at room temperature.

**TO SERVE:** Spoon the fruit salad into bowls and top with the mascarpone and hazelnuts.

Serves 6

# Onion, ricotta and sage omelette

30 ml olive oil

3 red onions, sliced

5 ml crushed garlic

30 ml chopped fresh sage
    or coriander

10 jumbo eggs, beaten

5 ml salt crystals

2 ml freshly ground black pepper

80 g ricotta cheese, drained
    and crumbled

20 g wild rocket, for serving

Preheat the oven grill to hot.

Heat the olive oil in a 25-cm, non-stick, heavy-based ovenproof frying pan and sauté the onions, garlic and sage until soft and the onions are golden in colour. Pour the eggs into the onion mixture, season with the salt and pepper, and top with the cheese. Cook over medium heat for 3–5, minutes or until almost set. Remove from the stove top and place under the grill for 3–5 minutes, or until golden in colour.

**TO SERVE:** Slice into wedges and garnish with the rocket.

Serves 6

# Smoked haddock quiche

**MAKE AHEAD:** The pastry can be made 1 day ahead.

SHORTCRUST PASTRY
225 g cake flour
125 g butter or margarine
2.5 ml salt
45 ml cold water

FILLING
30 ml cooking oil
6 leeks, thinly sliced
500 g smoked haddock, cooked
100 g Gruyère cheese, grated
5 egg yolks
350 ml fresh cream
1 strand saffron
2 ml white pepper

**TO MAKE THE PASTRY:** Sift the flour into a chilled mixing bowl. Rub in the margarine, add the salt and water, and mix. Knead the pastry until smooth, then shape into a ball. Wrap in clingfilm and refrigerate for 30 minutes, or until ready to use.

Preheat the oven to 200 °C. Coat a 26-cm, round pie dish with cooking spray and line the base and sides with the pastry (press it in with your fingers). Bake blind for 15 minutes. Set aside to cool.

**TO MAKE THE FILLING:** Reduce the oven temperature to 180 °C. Heat the oil in a heavy-based frying pan and sauté the leeks until tender. Arrange the leeks and haddock over the pastry case and top with the cheese. Combine the remaining ingredients in a mixing bowl and pour over the haddock mixture. Bake for 30 minutes.

Serves 6

# Sweetcorn blini with crème fraîche and salmon caviar

500 g fresh corn kernels cut from the cob
2 jumbo eggs
125 g cake flour
5 ml baking powder
5 ml salt
2 ml white pepper
80 ml cooking oil
250 g crème fraîche, for serving
100 g salmon caviar, for serving
15 ml chopped fresh dill, for serving

Blend the corn kernels, eggs, flour, baking powder, salt and pepper in the bowl of a food processor (fitted with the metal blade) until almost smooth. Heat the oil in a non-stick, heavy-based frying pan. Add spoonfuls of the batter and cook for 2–3 minutes over medium heat until the underside is golden. Flip and cook for a further 2–3 minutes, or until the blini is cooked. Remove from the heat and keep warm in the warming drawer. Repeat with the remaining mixture.

**TO SERVE:** Serve topped with the crème fraîche, salmon caviar and dill.

Makes 30

# Roast beef with blue cheese and green peppercorn topping

**MAKE AHEAD:** The topping can be made 1 day ahead. Refrigerate until ready to use.

2 kg sirloin of beef
10–15 ml salt
2 ml freshly ground black pepper
50 ml olive oil
10 ml crushed garlic

BLUE CHEESE AND GREEN
PEPPERCORN TOPPING
250 ml sour cream
60 g Madagascan green
    peppercorns, crushed
250 g creamy blue cheese, crumbled
30 ml fresh lemon juice
2 ml freshly ground black pepper

Preheat the oven to 180 °C. Coat a rack and a roasting pan with cooking spray and set aside.

Season the meat with the salt, pepper, olive oil and garlic. Transfer to the prepared pan, fat side uppermost. Spread the topping over the meat and roast until the required degree of doneness.

Remove from the oven and place in the warming drawer for 5–10 minutes before carving.

**TO MAKE THE TOPPING:** Combine all the ingredients in a mixing bowl.

**TO SERVE:** Carve the beef into slices and serve with the Polenta Flatbread (see opposite) on the side.

Serves 6

**CHEF'S NOTE:** Underdone or rare – 15 minutes per 500 g, plus an extra 15 minutes; or an internal temperature of 60 °C if using a meat thermometer. Medium – 20 minutes per 500 g, plus an extra 20 minutes; or an internal temperature of 70 °C.

# Polenta flatbread

35 g polenta, for dusting
1 x 10 g packet instant dry yeast
5 ml white sugar
300 ml lukewarm water
400 g cake flour
100 g polenta
10 ml salt crystals
15 ml chopped fresh rosemary
100 ml olive oil

Preheat the oven to 230 °C. Coat 2 baking sheets (39 x 26 cm) with cooking spray and sprinkle with 25 g polenta and set aside.

Combine the yeast, sugar and water in a bowl and set aside for 10 minutes until frothy. Sift the flour into a large mixing bowl and add the 100 g polenta, salt and rosemary. Make a well in the centre and pour in the yeast mixture, and the oil. Mix thoroughly. Turn the dough out onto a lightly floured surface and knead for 10 minutes, then shape into a ball. Place in a large bowl and cover with clingfilm. Leave to rise in a warm place until the dough has doubled in size.

Turn the dough out onto a lightly floured surface and punch down to remove any air bubbles. Divide it into 2 pieces and roll out to 3 mm thick. Sprinkle with the remaining 10 g polenta and prick with a fork. Place onto the prepared baking sheets, cover with clingfilm and set aside in a warm place for 15 minutes to prove. Bake for 10–15 minutes, or until golden brown in colour. Turn out onto a wire rack to cool.

Serves 6

# Chocolate-filled French toast

3 jumbo eggs
200 ml milk
15 ml castor sugar
8 slices white bread, thinly sliced
100 g milk chocolate, melted
40 g butter
15 ml cooking oil
100 g fresh raspberries, for serving
15 ml icing sugar, for serving

Using a balloon whisk, combine the eggs, milk and castor sugar in a medium-sized mixing bowl. Soak the bread in the egg mixture. Spread 4 slices of the bread with half the melted chocolate and stack on top of one another. Heat the butter and oil in a large, non-stick, heavy-based frying pan and place the prepared bread in it. Cook for 2 minutes on each side until golden in colour. Remove from the pan and keep warm in the warming drawer. Repeat with the remaining ingredients.

**TO SERVE:** Slice the French toast into fingers, top with the raspberries and dust with the icing sugar.

Serves 6

# Berry fruit sorbet

**MAKE AHEAD:** The sorbet can be made up to 3 days ahead.

800 g mixed frozen berries, thawed
    and liquidised
250 ml berry fruit juice
40 g white sugar
15 ml fresh lemon juice

Coat a plastic mould with cooking spray and set aside.

Spoon all the ingredients into the chilled bowl of an ice cream maker and churn for 20 minutes, or until the mixture thickens. Pour it into the prepared mould and freeze until ready to serve. If not using an ice cream machine, spoon the ingredients into the bowl of a food processor (fitted with the plastic blade), mix until thickened, then pour into the mould and freeze.

**TO SERVE:** Scoop into chilled glasses.

Serves 6

**CHEF'S NOTE:** Sorbet is softer and more granular than ice cream as it does not contain any fat or egg yolk. Do not beat sorbet during the freezing process.

Opposite, clockwise from top left:
Enjoy the feeling of crunchy sand under bare feet;
For a place card with a difference, write the guests' names on flat pebbles and arrange on a folded napkin;
To make a serviette ring, thread sea shells and stone-coloured beads onto wire and tie around a napkin;
Arrange an assortment of pots to create a display.

Right: Design a centrepiece using cylindrical vases of different sizes, filled with pebbles, broken sea shells and succulents.

**Top right:** Print out the menu and paste it onto decorative paper and cardboard, then tie onto the back of the chair.

**Bottom right:** Pour drinks into carafes and display on a tray together with glasses and a vase.

**Opposite:** Combine interesting design elements to create an inviting place setting and table.

# Spring lunch

Watercress soup

Old-fashioned granadilla lemonade

Roast pepper salad

Baked Scottish salmon with noodles and crispy cabbage

White chocolate pannacotta

Orange-poached plums

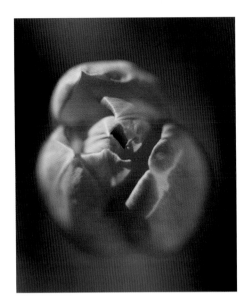

# Watercress soup

**MAKE AHEAD:** The soup can be made 1 day ahead. If so, refrigerate until ready to use.

50 ml olive oil
10 leeks, sliced
8 spring onions, snipped
2 potatoes, peeled and cubed
400 g fresh watercress
15 ml fresh lemon juice
5 ml salt
1 litre vegetable stock (10 ml stock powder dissolved in
    1 litre boiling water)
2 ml freshly ground black pepper

Heat the olive oil in a large, heavy-based saucepan and sauté the leeks, spring onions and potatoes until golden in colour. Add the watercress, lemon juice, salt and stock. Reduce the heat, cover and simmer for 25 minutes, or until tender. Remove from the heat and purée the soup in a food processor (fitted with the metal blade). Season to taste with the black pepper.

**TO SERVE:** Spoon into bowls and serve hot or cold.

Serves 6

**CHEF'S NOTE:** Soup can be frozen and thawed in the fridge overnight. However, freezing will cause the soup to lose a little of its colour, but not its flavour.

# Old-fashioned granadilla lemonade

**MAKE AHEAD:** The lemonade can be made up to 2 days ahead.

juice of 10 lemons, strained
pulp from 3 granadillas or 60 ml
    canned pulp
1.5 litres water
200 g white sugar
ice cubes, for serving
slices of lemon, for serving
Maraschino cherries with stems,
    for serving

Combine the lemon juice, granadilla pulp, water and sugar in a bowl and stir until the sugar has dissolved. Refrigerate until ready to serve.

**TO SERVE:** Serve well chilled over ice and decorate with lemon slices and cherries.

Serves 6

# Roast pepper salad

3 red peppers, halved and seeded
3 yellow peppers, halved and seeded
15 ml cooking oil
1 English cucumber, julienned
1 red onion, chopped
400 g cherry tomatoes, halved
100 ml snipped fresh watercress
500 ml fresh wild rocket

DRESSING
30 ml Dijon mustard
30 ml red wine vinegar
10 ml golden brown sugar
1 ml salt
100 ml olive oil

Preheat the oven to 220 °C.

Coat a roasting pan with cooking spray. Place the peppers in the prepared pan, drizzle with the oil and roast for 30 minutes. Remove from the oven, leave to cool, then pull off the skins and slice. Place the peppers and remaining ingredients in a bowl.

**TO MAKE THE DRESSING:** Combine the mustard, vinegar, sugar and salt in a small bowl. Whisk in the olive oil and set aside until ready to use.

**TO SERVE:** Spoon over the dressing and serve.

Serves 6

# Baked Scottish salmon with noodles and crispy cabbage

SALMON

6 x 200 g fillets Scottish or
    Norwegian salmon
45 ml olive oil
15 ml salt crystals
15 ml wholegrain mustard

CRISPY CABBAGE

20 ml cooking oil
350 g baby white cabbage, sliced
3 ml salt
10 ml white sugar

NOODLES

500 g ribbon egg noodles
15 ml sesame or peanut oil
45 ml light soy sauce
100 ml snipped fresh chives
100 ml chopped fresh coriander
2 carrots, peeled and finely chopped
200 g mangetout, blanched

Preheat the oven to 200 °C.

Coat an ovenproof dish with cooking spray. Place the fillets in the prepared dish and season with the oil, salt and mustard. Bake for 30 minutes, or until cooked. Remove from the oven and set aside until ready to serve.

**TO MAKE THE CABBAGE:** Heat the oil in a wok or large, heavy-based frying pan. Add the cabbage and fry for 2–3 minutes, or until frizzled and golden. Remove from the heat and add the salt and sugar.

**TO MAKE THE NOODLES:** Boil the noodles in a large saucepan of salted boiling water until *al dente*. Drain and toss in the remaining ingredients.

**TO SERVE:** Spoon the noodles onto individual plates, top with the salmon and sprinkle the cabbage over.

Serves 6

# White chocolate pannacotta

**MAKE AHEAD:** The pannacotta can be made 1 day ahead. Keep refrigerated until ready to serve.

4 sheets gelatine
600 ml fresh cream
150 ml milk
60 g castor sugar
200 g good-quality white chocolate,
　　broken into pieces

Coat a mould or individual cups with cooking spray and set aside.

Soak the gelatine sheets in a plate of cold water until soft, then set aside until ready to use. Heat the cream, milk and castor sugar in a heavy-based saucepan over low heat to melt the sugar, stirring occasionally. When the cream starts to bubble up the sides of the saucepan, remove from the heat and stir in the chocolate until melted. Drain the excess water off the gelatine and add the gelatine to the cream mixture. Stir until dissolved. Pour the mixture into the prepared mould or cups and refrigerate overnight or for at least 6 hours. The pannacotta should still have a slight wobble when ready to serve.

**TO SERVE:** Unmould onto a serving platter or plates and serve.

Serves 6

# Orange-poached plums

**MAKE AHEAD:** This dessert can be made up to 2 days ahead. Keep refrigerated but bring to room temperature before serving.

12 fresh red plums
200 g white sugar
500 ml water
grated rind of 1 orange
1 stick cinnamon

Rinse the plums and, using a skewer, prick each plum twice and set aside.

Bring the sugar and water to the boil in a large, heavy-based saucepan, stirring until the sugar has dissolved. Add the orange rind, cinnamon and plums and simmer for 5 minutes, or until the fruit is tender. Remove from the heat, discard the rind and cinnamon stick and leave the plums to cool in the syrup.

**TO SERVE:** Spoon into a bowl and serve at room temperature.

Serves 6

From top left, clockwise:
Arrange cut tulips in a container filled
with oasis and cover with moss;
Arrange bunched flowers in different glass
vases and display on a console table;
Sip drinks served from a butlers tray whilst
relaxing on a cotton throw and cushions;
Create a colourful feature by grouping
containers filled with miniature daffodils.

**Opposite top:** Combining different textures and colours of tableware, glassware, fruits and flowers engages the senses.

**Opposite bottom, left and right:** Beautiful crockery and fresh flowers enhance the table setting.

**Above left:** Layer plates with different designs on a folded napkin to define the place setting.

**Above right:** A display of cut crystal glassware.

# Cocktail party

Fruity cocktail

Nut and seed mix

Anchovy and garlic grissini

Beef carpaccio in phyllo pastry

Vegetarian rice wraps

Double-salmon fishcakes with mayonnaise

Sesame-crusted seared tuna

Brandy snaps

Balsamic strawberries

# Fruity cocktail

750 ml dry white wine
200 ml peach juice
250 ml apple juice
4 fresh peaches, stoned and sliced
500 g fresh raspberries
juice of 4 limes
juice of 3 oranges
100 ml Cognac
500 ml sparkling water
30 ml golden brown sugar
ice cubes, for serving

Combine all the ingredients in a large bowl and stir. Cover and refrigerate for a minimum of 2 hours, or up to 12 hours, to blend the flavours.

**TO SERVE:** Fill the glasses with ice, pour over the cocktail mixture and serve immediately.

Serves 12

# Nut and seed mix

**MAKE AHEAD:** The nut and seed mix can be made up to 2 days ahead, but store in an airtight container.

300 g pumpkin seeds
200 g sunflower seeds
200 g sesame seeds
250 g pine nuts
300 g roasted peanuts
300 g dried cranberries

Preheat the oven to 180 °C. Coat a roasting pan with cooking spray and set aside.

Combine all the ingredients in a large mixing bowl. Transfer to the prepared pan. Bake for 10 minutes. Remove the pan from the oven and stir, return to the oven and bake for a further 10 minutes or until the mixture is light brown in colour.

**TO SERVE:** Spoon into serving bowls.

Serves 12

# Anchovy and garlic grissini

**MAKE AHEAD:** The grissini can be made 1 day ahead and crisped in a warm oven for 5 minutes before serving.

2 heads garlic
200 g white bread flour
100 g wholewheat flour
5 ml salt
1 x 10 g packet instant dry yeast
200 ml lukewarm water
30 ml olive oil
30 g butter, softened
16 anchovy fillets in oil, drained and
    halved lengthwise
45 ml olive oil, for brushing

Preheat the oven to 200 °C.

Coat 3 baking sheets with cooking spray and set aside.

Place the heads of garlic on one of the prepared sheets and roast for 20 minutes. Remove from the oven and set aside to cool. Peel the garlic cloves, cut into pieces and set aside.

Combine the flours, salt and yeast in a large mixing bowl. Make a well in the centre and add the water, oil and butter. Mix thoroughly. Turn the dough out onto a lightly floured surface and knead for 10 minutes or until it is smooth and pliable. Shape the dough into a ball, place it in a large bowl and cover with clingfilm, then set aside in a warm place to rise until it has doubled in size.

Turn the dough out onto a lightly floured surface and punch down to remove any air bubbles. Cut it into 24 pieces and shape each piece into a grissini, 20 x 1 cm in diameter. Flatten the dough, place 3 pieces of garlic and 3 pieces of anchovy alternately down the centre of each grissini. Pinch the dough to cover the garlic and anchovy, then reshape. Cut each grissini in half.

Place the grissini onto the prepared sheets, cover with clingfilm and set aside in a warm place to prove for 15 minutes. Remove the clingfilm and brush the tops of the grissini with the oil and bake for 5 minutes. Remove from the oven, brush with the remaining oil and bake for a further 3 minutes, or until golden brown in colour. Turn out onto a wire rack to cool.

Makes 48

# Beef carpaccio in phyllo pastry

4 sheets phyllo pastry

50 g butter, melted, for brushing

500 ml cooking oil

24 slices beef carpaccio, cut into
    thin strips

1 fresh pear, quartered

30 g snipped fresh chives, for serving

200 ml cranberry or quince jelly,
    for serving

Brush each sheet of the pastry with the butter and place on top of one another on a board. Cut the pastry stack into 4 equal lengths and 3 equal widths, making 12 squares. Shape each square into a cone and refrigerate until ready to use. Remove the pastry from the fridge and heat the cooking oil in a large, heavy-based saucepan. Deep-fry the cones until golden in colour, then drain on paper towel.

**TO SERVE:** Spoon the carpaccio and pear into the fried cones and top with the chives and jelly.

Serves 12

# Vegetarian rice wraps

1 small green cabbage, shredded
4 beetroot, peeled and shredded
2 red peppers, seeded and julienned
2 carrots, peeled and julienned
12 pieces pickled ginger, drained
12 sheets Asian rice paper
250 ml sweet chilli sauce, for serving
50 g pickled ginger, for serving

Place the prepared vegetables in small, individual mixing bowls and set aside. Soften the rice paper in very hot water and lie flat on a damp tea towel. Spoon a little of each of the vegetables into the centre of the rice paper and roll up, folding the sides into a cone shape. Transfer the wraps to a board, cover with a damp tea towel and refrigerate until ready to serve.

**TO SERVE:** Serve with the sweet chilli sauce and the ginger on the side.

Serves 12

# Double-salmon fishcakes with mayonnaise

**MAKE AHEAD:** Prepare the fishcakes 1 day ahead and refrigerate until ready to bake on the day.

200 g fresh Scottish or Norwegian
  salmon, filleted
100 g smoked salmon, chopped
400 g mashed potato
1 jumbo egg
1 onion, chopped
25 ml chopped fresh Italian parsley
25 ml chopped fresh chives
5 ml salt
15 ml fresh lemon juice
50 g smoked salmon, for serving
fresh chives, for serving
wedges fresh lime, for serving

MAYONNAISE
200 ml mayonnaise
150 ml crème fraîche or sour cream
30 ml chopped fresh chives

Preheat the oven to 180 °C. Coat 2 ovenproof dishes with cooking spray and set aside.

Place the fillets in one of the prepared dishes, cover with clingfilm and microwave at 100% power for 2 minutes. Using a slotted spoon, transfer to a mixing bowl. Add the remaining ingredients (except the salmon, chives and limes for serving) and mash thoroughly with a potato masher. Refrigerate for 30 minutes. Remove from the fridge and shape into round, flat patties. Transfer to the second prepared dish and bake for 25–30 minutes, or until cooked. Keep warm until ready to serve, then arrange on a serving platter.

**TO MAKE THE MAYONNAISE:** Combine all the ingredients in a small bowl and refrigerate until ready to use.

**TO SERVE:** Arrange the fishcakes on a serving platter, top with the salmon and chives, and serve with the lime wedges and mayonnaise on the side.

Makes 24

# Sesame-crusted seared tuna

2 x 250 g fresh tuna loin, trimmed
50 ml sesame oil
10 ml fresh lemon juice
50 ml black sesame seeds
5 ml salt crystals
soy sauce, for serving
slices or wedges fresh lime,
  for serving
fresh coriander, for serving

Coat the tuna with the oil and lemon juice, then crust with the sesame seeds and salt. Heat a non-stick, heavy-based frying pan and sear the tuna for 1 minute on each side. Remove from the heat and refrigerate until ready to serve. Transfer to a board and slice into bite-sized pieces.

**TO SERVE:** Arrange on a serving platter and serve with the soy sauce, lime slices or wedges and coriander on the side.

Serves 12

# Brandy snaps

BRANDY SNAPS
100 g butter
100 g castor sugar
60 ml golden syrup
5 ml brandy
100 g cake flour
5 ml ground ginger

FILLING
250 ml fresh cream
15 ml brandy
15 ml icing sugar
2 ml ground cinnamon
2 ml ground ginger

**CHEF'S NOTE:** Brandy snaps may be left unrolled and stacked with the filling in between.

Preheat the oven to 160 °C. Line 2 baking sheets with baking paper and set aside.

**TO MAKE THE BRANDY SNAPS:** Place the butter, castor sugar, syrup and brandy in a small, heavy-based saucepan. Melt over low heat, but do not boil. Stir in the flour and ginger until smooth. Remove from the heat and drop teaspoonfuls of the mixture onto the prepared sheets, allowing sufficient space in between for spreading. Bake for 8–9 minutes, or until golden brown in colour. Set aside to cool slightly.

Lift each brandy snap from the sheet using a spatula and wrap around the handle of a wooden spoon. Once firm, remove from the handle and place on a wire rack to harden.

**TO MAKE THE FILLING:** Whip the cream until stiff and stir in the remaining ingredients. Fill each brandy snap with the ginger cream.

**TO SERVE:** Arrange the brandy snaps on a serving platter, pipe a star of cream onto one end of each snap and serve with the Balsamic Strawberries on the side.

Makes 24

# Balsamic strawberries

500 g strawberries, halved
15 ml balsamic vinegar
60 ml icing sugar, for serving

Place the strawberries in a bowl and coat with the vinegar. Dust them with the icing sugar.

**Above left:** String Chinese lanterns for accent lighting.

**Above right:** Ostrich feathers create a sense of occasion.

**Right:** Set the scene by placing a crab apple into each glass and topping up with champagne.

**Opposite:** Arrange ostrich feathers in tall glass vases as a focal point on cocktail tables.

This page: Colour accents and the use of lighting add to the atmosphere.

**Top left:** Before serving drinks, scatter rose petals

between the glasses on the tray.

**Bottom left:** Combine the design elements to create an inviting setting.

# Formal winter dinner

Cauliflower soup

Lettuce wedges with anchovy dressing

Roast steak

Sweet potato and coriander mash

Tian of roast vegetables

Glazed baby onions

Grand Marnier soufflé

**CHEF'S NOTE:** Soup can be frozen and thawed in the fridge overnight.

# Cauliflower soup

**MAKE AHEAD:** Make the soup 2 days ahead if necessary and refrigerate. Reheat before serving..

50 ml olive oil
4 leeks, thinly sliced
8 celery stalks, sliced
5 ml crushed garlic
1.5 kg fresh cauliflower, roughly chopped
1.5 litres vegetable stock (30 ml stock powder mixed with
    1.5 litres boiling water)
100 ml fresh cream
5 ml salt crystals
2 ml white pepper
10 ml truffle oil
ciabatta, sliced and toasted, for serving

Heat the oil in a large, heavy-based saucepan and sauté the leeks, celery, garlic and cauliflower until golden in colour. Add the stock and bring to the boil. Reduce the heat and simmer, covered, until the vegetables are tender. Remove from the heat and set aside to cool. Add the cream and season with the salt, pepper and truffle oil. Blend the soup in a food processor (fitted with the metal blade) until smooth. Return the soup to the saucepan and reheat.

**TO SERVE:** Spoon into bowls and serve with the toast on the side.

Serves 6

# Lettuce wedges with anchovy dressing

**MAKE AHEAD:** The dressing can be made and refrigerated 1 day ahead.

1 fresh iceberg lettuce, outer leaves removed and cut into 6 wedges
3 hard-boiled eggs, peeled and quartered
2 plum tomatoes, sliced
30 ml capers, drained

ANCHOVY DRESSING
150 ml olive oil
1 jumbo egg
5 ml crushed garlic
3 anchovy fillets, drained
30 ml fresh lemon juice
100 ml grated Parmesan cheese
2 ml salt

Place the lettuce wedges on a serving platter. Top with the eggs, tomatoes and capers, then refrigerate.

**TO MAKE THE DRESSING:** Blend all the ingredients in the bowl of a food processor (fitted with the metal blade) and refrigerate until ready to use.

**TO SERVE:** Spoon the dressing over the salad and serve.

Serves 6

# Roast steak

**MAKE AHEAD:** Place the steak in the marinade 1 day ahead and refrigerate.

1.5 kg rump or sirloin steak, 5 cm thick
5 ml salt crystals
5 ml coarsely ground black pepper
100 ml dry red wine

MARINADE
100 ml olive oil
100 ml soy sauce
30 ml red wine vinegar
30 ml balsamic vinegar
10 ml crushed garlic

**TO MAKE THE MARINADE:** Combine all the marinade ingredients in a large, non-metallic bowl. Marinate the steak and refrigerate for at least 3 hours, or overnight. Remove the meat from the fridge and bring to room temperature.

Preheat the oven to 230 °C.

Coat a rack and a roasting pan with cooking spray. Remove the steak from the marinade and place on the prepared rack, fat side uppermost. Season with the salt and pepper and roast for 10 minutes. Remove from the oven, pour the red wine over and baste the steak with the pan juices. Roast for a further 20 minutes. Remove from the oven and transfer to a warming drawer for 10 minutes.

**TO SERVE:** Carve into thin slices and serve with Sweet Potato and Coriander Mash, Tian of Roast Vegetables and Glazed Baby Onions.

Serves 6

# Sweet potato and coriander mash

1.5 kg sweet potatoes, peeled and cut into chunks
5 ml salt
50 ml chopped fresh coriander

In a large, heavy-based saucepan, boil the potatoes in salted boiling water until tender. Drain, then return the potatoes to the saucepan and add the coriander. Mash until smooth.

Serves 6

# Tian of roast vegetables

700 g brinjals (aubergines), cut into
    5 mm slices
2 large potatoes, peeled and thinly
    sliced
350 g baby marrows (courgettes),
    ends removed and sliced
4 plum tomatoes, sliced
100 g Gruyère cheese, sliced
125 ml olive oil
10 ml crushed garlic
50 ml chopped fresh parsley
50 ml chopped fresh basil
5 ml salt

Preheat the oven to 190 °C.

Coat 6 ovenproof ramekins with cooking spray. Layer the vegetables and cheese in the prepared ramekins. Combine the oil, garlic, parsley, basil and salt in a small bowl and pour over the vegetables. Bake for 30 minutes, or until the vegetables are tender and browned around the edges. Keep warm until ready to serve.

Serves 6

# Glazed baby onions

24 baby onions
30 ml olive oil
2 ml salt
30 ml golden brown sugar

In a large, heavy-based saucepan, boil the onions in salted boiling water for 10 minutes. Remove from the heat and drain. Heat the oil in the same saucepan. Add the onions, salt and sugar and sauté until tender and golden in colour.

Serves 6

**CHEF'S NOTE:** For extra zing, add 30 ml balsamic vinegar to the onions while sautéing.

# Grand Marnier® soufflé

10 ml butter, for greasing
20 ml white sugar, for coating
60 g butter
60 g cake flour
250 ml milk
5 ml vanilla essence
90 g white sugar
4 jumbo egg yolks
50 ml Grand Marnier liqueur
6 jumbo egg whites
icing sugar, for serving

Preheat the oven to 190 °C.

Coat six 9-cm diameter soufflé dishes with the butter and sugar, place on a baking sheet and set aside.

Melt the butter in a heavy-based saucepan and add the flour. Cook for 1 minute, stirring continuously. Remove from the heat and add the milk, vanilla and sugar. Return to the stove top over medium heat and stir continuously until the mixture boils and thickens. Remove the saucepan from the heat. Beat the egg yolks in a mixing bowl, spoon the milk mixture into the eggs and stir. Add the liqueur. Using an electric beater, whisk the egg whites until stiff peaks form. Gently fold the egg whites into the mixture with a metal spoon. Spoon the mixture into the prepared dishes and bake for 20–25 minutes, or until puffed.

**TO SERVE:** Dust with the icing sugar and serve immediately.

Makes 6

**This page and opposite:** Nothing sets the mood quite like flowers, candles and lighting.

**This page and opposite:** Combine an array of sumptious crockery, glassware and beautiful flowers, using warm colours such as red, orange and gold.

# Grilling party

Pear, walnut and watercress salad

Grilled line fish fillets with coriander pesto

Curried lamb potjie

Courgette pickle

Fruity chicken

Braai sandwiches

Ma's peach chutney

Buttermilk pudding

Helen's macadamia and coffee biscotti

# Pear, walnut and watercress salad

**MAKE AHEAD:** Make the dressing 1 day ahead and refrigerate until ready to use.

3 fresh ripe pears, quartered
    and sliced
150 g whole walnuts
250 g fresh watercress
200 g Parmesan cheese, sliced

DRESSING
200 ml olive oil
100 ml white balsamic vinegar
2 ml salt
5 ml mustard powder
10 ml white sugar

Combine all the salad ingredients in a bowl and refrigerate.

**TO MAKE THE DRESSING:** Blend all the ingredients in the bowl of a food processor (fitted with the metal blade) and refrigerate until ready to use.

**TO SERVE:** Spoon the dressing over the salad and serve.

Serves 6

# Grilled line fish fillets with coriander pesto

**MAKE AHEAD:** Make the pesto 1 day ahead and refrigerate.

6 x 200 g line fish fillets
30 ml olive oil
7 ml salt crystals
3 ml freshly ground black pepper

CORIANDER PESTO
4 fresh hot chillies, seeded
    and chopped
15 ml crushed garlic
200 g pine nuts
30 g fresh coriander
1 ml salt
200 ml cooking oil

Prepare an open charcoal fire.

Slash the fish fillets diagonally in 2 places, coat with the olive oil and season with the salt and pepper. Grill over medium coals for 10 minutes, turning frequently. Remove the fish from the heat and spread a spoonful of the pesto over each fillet. Return to the coals for 2 minutes. Remove from the heat.

**TO MAKE THE PESTO:** Blend the chillies, garlic, pine nuts, coriander and salt in the bowl of a food processor (fitted with the metal blade) until smooth. Gradually beat in the oil. Spoon into a small bowl and refrigerate until ready to use.

**TO SERVE:** Transfer the fish fillets to a serving platter and serve with the remaining pesto on the side.

Serves 6

**CHEF'S NOTE:** The fish fillets can also be wrapped in foil and cooked under the grill of an oven.

# Curried lamb potjie

25 ml cooking oil
12 slices neck of lamb, 2.5 cm thick
1 onion, sliced
10 ml crushed garlic
25 ml mild curry powder
50 ml chopped fresh root ginger
7 ml salt
2 ml freshly ground black pepper
500 ml meat stock (15 ml stock
    powder mixed with 500 ml
    boiling water)
250 ml apricot juice
12 baby onions
12 baby potatoes, peeled
300 g baby carrots, peeled
500 g mixed dried fruit

Prepare an open charcoal fire.

Heat the cooking oil in a three-legged pot over the fire and brown the meat. Add the onion, garlic, curry powder and ginger, and sauté. Season with the salt and pepper. Add the heated stock and apricot juice, cover with the lid and simmer for 2 hours, or until the meat is tender. Remove from the heat, add the remaining ingredients and return to the fire. Simmer, covered, until the vegetables are cooked and the fruit is tender.

**TO SERVE:** Serve the lamb potjie with rice and the Courgette Pickle.

Serves 6

**CHEF'S NOTE:** Curry powder is sautéed with onion and garlic to develop its flavour. Economical cuts of meat containing a lot of sinew, such as neck, shin and chuck, are most suitable for potjiekos. Simmering for a long time develops the gelatine and enhances the flavour.

# Courgette pickle

**MAKE AHEAD:** This pickle can be made and refrigerated up to 5 days ahead.

1 kg courgettes (baby marrows),
    sliced
1 red onion, sliced
1 red pepper, seeded and julienned
50 ml salt crystals
10 ml crushed garlic
5 ml chopped fresh chillies
250 ml white wine vinegar
50 g golden brown sugar
2 ml ground turmeric
10 ml mustard seeds
10 ml cumin seeds

Combine all the ingredients in a large, heavy-based saucepan and bring to the boil. Cover and simmer for 3 minutes. Remove from the heat and set aside to cool. Transfer to sterilised jars and refrigerate until ready to use.

Serves 6

# Fruity chicken

**MAKE AHEAD:** Make the marinade and marinate the chicken 1 day ahead in the fridge.

6 chicken thighs

6 chicken breasts

500 ml meat stock (10 ml stock
    powder mixed with 500 ml
    boiling water)

MARINADE

100 ml avocado oil

50 ml brandy

50 ml plum sauce

50 ml teriyaki sauce

15 ml soy sauce

2 ml salt

2 ml freshly ground black pepper

Preheat the oven to 200 °C.

Coat an ovenproof dish with cooking spray. Place the chicken pieces in the prepared dish. Pour the heated stock over and poach for 10 minutes in the oven. Remove from the heat and set aside to cool. Transfer the chicken pieces to the marinade and refrigerate for 3 hours or overnight, then take out of the fridge and bring to room temperature.

Prepare an open charcoal fire. Remove the chicken pieces from the marinade and grill slowly over medium coals for 10 minutes per side, or until cooked, turning frequently. Baste with the marinade.

**TO MAKE THE MARINADE:** Combine all the marinade ingredients in a large, non-metallic bowl and set aside until ready to use.

Serves 6

# Braai sandwiches

12 slices white bread

100 g butter or margarine, softened

2 red onions, sliced

3 tomatoes, sliced

5 ml salt

2 ml freshly ground black pepper

Prepare an open charcoal fire.

Coat a hinged grid with cooking spray and set aside.

Spread the bread on both sides with the butter or margarine. Top 6 slices of the bread with the onions and tomatoes. Season with the salt and pepper. Top with the remaining slices of bread and transfer the sandwiches to the prepared grid. Grill slowly over low coals until golden in colour. Remove from the grid and keep warm in the warming drawer until ready to serve.

**TO SERVE:** Serve with Ma's Peach Chutney on the side.

Serves 6

# Ma's peach chutney

**MAKE AHEAD:** This chutney can be made up to 7 days ahead. Refrigerate until ready to use.

1.5 kg yellow peaches, peeled,
    stoned and sliced

4 onions, chopped

1 clove garlic, peeled

500 g sultanas

500 g dried apricots, sliced

1 kg caramel brown sugar

5 ml salt

2 ml white pepper

2 ml ground ginger

2 ml cayenne pepper

750 ml brown vinegar

Combine all the ingredients in a large, heavy-based saucepan and bring to the boil. Cover and simmer for 2–2½ hours, or until the fruit is tender. Remove from the heat and set aside to cool. Transfer to sterilised jars and refrigerate until ready to use.

Makes 7 litres

# Buttermilk pudding

**MAKE AHEAD:** Make this pudding 1 day ahead and refrigerate until ready to serve.

200 g castor sugar

250 ml fresh cream

2 ml vanilla essence

15 ml gelatine powder, soaked in
    30 ml cold water

500 ml buttermilk

30 ml fresh granadilla pulp,
    for serving

15 ml grated orange rind, for serving

Coat a decorative mould with cooking spray and set aside.

Combine the castor sugar, cream and vanilla essence in a small, heavy-based saucepan. Stir over low heat until the sugar dissolves, then bring to the boil. Remove from the heat. Stir in the gelatine and set aside to cool. Stir in the buttermilk and mix thoroughly. Pour into the prepared mould and refrigerate for at least 3 hours, or until ready to serve.

**TO SERVE:** Top with the granadilla pulp and orange rind.

Serves 6

# Helen's macadamia and coffee biscotti

**MAKE AHEAD:** Make the biscotti up to 3 days ahead and store in an airtight container.

50 g espresso coffee beans

400 g cake flour

7 ml baking powder

100 g butter

220 g castor sugar

150 g macadamia nuts, toasted and
    coarsely chopped

25 ml strong, freshly brewed coffee

2 jumbo eggs

Preheat the oven to 180 °C. Line 2 baking sheets with baking paper. Coat the sheets with cooking spray and set aside.

Coarsely grind the coffee beans in the bowl of a food processor (fitted with the metal blade). Add the flour, baking powder, butter and castor sugar and mix to form a scone-like dough. Add the nuts. Transfer the dough to a mixing bowl and mix in the coffee and eggs. Turn the dough out onto a lightly floured surface and shape into two 20 x 8 x 2-cm rectangles. Place the rectangles onto one of the prepared sheets and bake for 40 minutes, or until a skewer inserted into the centre comes out clean. Allow to cool completely.

Using a serrated knife, cut into 2.5-cm-thick slices. Arrange the biscotti on the other prepared sheet and bake for 8 minutes. Remove from the oven, turn the biscotti over and bake for a further 8 minutes, or until dry. Allow to cool, then store in an airtight container.

Makes 30

This page and opposite: To give the African scene a chic twist, hang cylindrical shades with lights, and include other decorative elements with traditional woven baskets.

**This page and opposite:** It's relatively simple to create an African theme if you keep to natural, earthy tones and textures.

# Picnic

Pita bread with vegetarian filling

Red onion marmalade

Steak sandwich

Mustard mayonnaise

Poached salmon

Cucumber and dill salad

Nectarine and cinnamon picnic cakes

Cherry and cashew nut nougat

# Pita bread with vegetarian filling

125 ml lukewarm water

1 x 10 g packet instant dry yeast

5 ml white sugar

500 g cake flour

2 ml salt

25 ml cooking oil

250 ml lukewarm water

15 ml chopped fresh mint, for serving

VEGETARIAN FILLING

1 small lettuce, shredded

1 English cucumber, chopped

6 radishes, sliced

1 green pepper, seeded and
    chopped

1 red pepper, seeded and chopped

6 spring onions, sliced

2 tomatoes, chopped

12 black olives, pitted and halved

100 g feta cheese, cubed

100 ml plain yoghurt

DRESSING

50 ml cooking oil

50 ml olive oil

15 ml fresh lemon juice

5 ml crushed garlic

15 ml chopped fresh mint

15 ml chopped fresh parsley

salt and pepper, to taste

Preheat the oven to 230 °C. Coat a 39 x 26 cm baking sheet with cooking spray and set aside.

Pour the 125 ml water into a bowl, sprinkle the yeast and sugar over and set aside until frothy. Sift the flour and salt into a large bowl. Make a well in the centre and pour in the yeast mixture. Add the oil and 250 ml water, then mix thoroughly. Turn the dough out onto a lightly floured surface and knead for 10 minutes. Place the dough in a large bowl, cover with clingfilm and set aside in a warm place to rise until it has doubled in size. Divide into 6 pieces, each the size of a tennis ball. Place on the prepared sheet and flatten into rounds. Bake for 8 minutes or until puffed and pale in colour. Remove from the oven and cover with a damp cloth until ready to use.

**TO MAKE THE FILLING:** Place the vegetables, cheese and yoghurt in a bowl.

**TO MAKE THE DRESSING:** Combine the ingredients in a small bowl, pour over the filling mixture and season to taste. Refrigerate until ready to use.

**TO SERVE:** Slit and halve the pitas and spoon in the filling. Garnish with fresh mint and serve with the Red Onion Marmalade.

Serves 6

# Red onion marmalade

**MAKE AHEAD:** Make the marmalade up to 3 days ahead, spoon into a sterilised container and refrigerate.

30 ml olive oil

6 red onions, sliced

5 ml salt

2 ml freshly ground black pepper

10 ml white sugar

50 ml balsamic vinegar

Heat the olive oil in a large, heavy-based saucepan and fry the onions until translucent. Add the remaining ingredients and bring to the boil. Reduce the heat, cover with the lid and simmer for 30 minutes. Remove from the heat and set aside to cool. The onions should be thick and resemble marmalade.

Serves 6

# Steak sandwich

**MAKE AHEAD:** Make the mayonnaise 1 day ahead if you like and refrigerate until ready to use.

3 x 200 g sirloin steak, 2.5 cm thick
3 ml salt crystals
1 ml freshly ground black pepper
200 g cherry tomatoes, halved
1 ciabatta bread, sliced and toasted
1 red onion, sliced
100 g fresh salad leaves, e.g. baby
    spinach, lettuce and watercress

Coat a heavy-based grilling pan with cooking spray and set aside.

Slash the fat edges of the steaks at 2.5 cm intervals to prevent curling during the grilling process. Heat the pan and grill the steaks for 2 minutes per side. Season with the salt and pepper. Remove from the heat, transfer to a board and cut into thin slices. Reheat the same grilling pan and grill the tomatoes until cooked. Remove from the heat and set aside.

**TO SERVE:** Spread half the slices of toasted bread with the Mustard Mayonnaise and place the steak, onion, tomatoes and the salad leaves on top. Finally, top each slice with another slice of bread and serve.

Serves 6

# Mustard mayonnaise

200 ml mayonnaise
30 ml wholegrain mustard
2 ml cayenne pepper

Combine all the ingredients in a small bowl and set aside until ready to use.

# Poached salmon

**MAKE AHEAD:** The broth can be made 1 day ahead and refrigerated.

6 x 200 g Scottish or Norwegian
    salmon fillets
3 limes, halved, for serving

BROTH
1 onion, sliced
3 fresh bay leaves
2 ml salt crystals
5 ml whole black peppercorns
250 ml white wine
500 ml water

Preheat the oven to 180 °C.

Coat an ovenproof dish with cooking spray. Place the fillets in the prepared dish. Pour over the broth and poach, uncovered, for 20 minutes or until cooked. Remove from the oven and cool in the broth for 20 minutes. Using a spatula, remove the fillets from the broth and set aside until ready to use.

**TO MAKE THE BROTH:** Combine all the ingredients in a large, heavy-based saucepan and bring to the boil. Cover and simmer for 10 minutes. Remove from the heat, strain and refrigerate until ready to use.

**TO SERVE:** Transfer the salmon to a serving platter and serve topped with Cucumber and Dill Salad, and the limes on the side.

Serves 6

# Cucumber and dill salad

2 English cucumbers, peeled, halved and sliced
100 ml white wine vinegar
15 ml chopped fresh dill
30 ml castor sugar

Place the cucumber in a serving dish. Combine the remaining ingredients together in a small bowl and pour over the cucumber. Refrigerate until ready to serve.

# Nectarine and cinnamon picnic cakes

**MAKE AHEAD:** For convenience, make these cakes 1 day ahead and store in an airtight container.

250 g cake flour

50 g ground almonds

10 ml baking powder

5 ml ground cinnamon

125 g butter or margarine

220 g golden brown sugar

5 ml vanilla essence

3 jumbo eggs

250 ml sour cream

2 ripe nectarines, stoned and sliced

25 ml golden brown sugar, for serving

Preheat the oven to 180 °C. Line 2 x 6-cup jumbo muffin tins with paper casings and set aside.

Sift the flour, almonds, baking powder and cinnamon into a mixing bowl and set aside. Cream the butter or margarine and sugar in the bowl of a food mixer until light and creamy. Add the vanilla essence and eggs and mix. Add the flour mixture and sour cream and beat thoroughly. Spoon the mixture into the paper casings. Top with the nectarine slices and sprinkle with the sugar.

Bake for 25 minutes, or until the tops of the cakes spring back when lightly touched. Remove from the oven and leave to cool in the tin for 10 minutes. Turn out onto a wire rack to cool.

Makes 9

**CHEF'S NOTE:** Plums may be substituted for the nectarines.

# Cherry and cashew nut nougat

**MAKE AHEAD:** The nougat can be made 1 day ahead.

4 sheets edible rice paper
525 g castor sugar
125 ml honey
50 ml golden syrup
250 ml water
2 jumbo egg whites
50 g cashew nuts
75 g glacé cherries
15 ml icing sugar, for dusting

Line a 26 x 18 cm baking tin with rice paper and set aside.

Combine the castor sugar, honey, syrup and water in a large, heavy-based saucepan over low heat until the sugar dissolves, then bring to the boil. Boil the syrup until the hard-crack stage. Alternatively, using a sugar thermometer, boil until 150–160 °C (depending on altitude). Remove from the heat. Using a food mixer beat the egg whites until stiff peaks begin to form. With the mixer running, pour in the hot syrup and beat for 2 minutes. Fold in the nuts and cherries. Spoon the nougat onto the rice paper and top with another layer of rice paper. Set aside in a cool place for at least 12 hours.

**TO SERVE:** Using a serrated knife, cut into bite-sized pieces and dust with the icing sugar.

Serves 6

**This page:** Arrange cutlery in a woven basket, tie rolled serviettes with colourful ribbon bands, and add a touch of whimsy to a bicycle with a basket of fresh flowers.

**Opposite:** Picnics can be fun and colourful. Decorate the area with an array of throws and pillows. Pack a picnic basket with delicious goodies and use ceramic crockery for a touch of class.

**Above left:** A galvanised bucket decorated with colourful ribbon becomes a novel wine cooler.

**Left:** Tuck cutlery into a simply folded napkin.

**Opposite:** Even picnics need a floral touch!

# Pool party

Plum and nectarine fizz

Baguette slices with balsamic dipping oil

Gazpacho

Chilled cucumber and avocado soup

Summer fish salad

Honey-roasted baby chickens

Mustard potato salad

Rhubarb and strawberry pudding
with cinnamon mascarpone

Chocolate-orange tarts

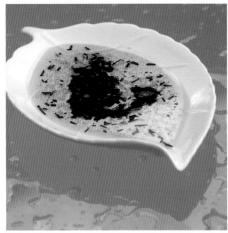

# Plum and nectarine fizz

3 plums, halved, stoned and thinly
    sliced
3 nectarines, halved, stoned and
    thinly sliced
375 ml peach nectar
50 ml orange liqueur
750 ml dry white wine, chilled
ice cubes, for serving
750 ml sparkling water, chilled

Combine all the ingredients, except the ice and sparkling water, in a large jug
and stir. Cover and refrigerate for at least 2 hours, or up to 12 hours, to blend
the flavours.

**TO SERVE:** Fill a jug with ice, add the fruit mixture and pour over the
sparking water. Serve immediately.

Serves 6

# Baguette slices with balsamic dipping oil

250 ml lemon-flavoured olive oil
100 ml balsamic vinegar
10 ml chopped fresh rosemary
5 ml crushed garlic
10 ml grated lemon rind
1 ml cayenne pepper
1 long French baguette, thinly sliced

Combine the olive oil, vinegar, rosemary, garlic, lemon rind and cayenne
pepper in a small bowl and set aside for 1 hour to blend the flavours.

**TO SERVE:** Arrange the baguette slices on a serving platter. Pour the oil into
a shallow bowl and place on the prepared platter for dipping.

Serves 6

# Gazpacho

**MAKE AHEAD:** Make the soup up to 2 days ahead and refrigerate until ready to serve.

6 x 410 g cans whole peeled
    tomatoes
250 ml tomato purée
2 cloves garlic, crushed
250 ml cooking oil
8 slices (no crusts) fresh white bread
juice and rind of 2 lemons
100 ml sherry or red wine vinegar
40 g caramel brown sugar
salt and freshly ground black pepper,
    to taste
1 ml Tabasco sauce
cucumber ribbons and Italian parsley,
    for serving

Purée the canned tomatoes with their juice in a food processor (fitted with the metal blade) until smooth, then set aside. Blend the tomato purée, garlic, cooking oil and bread until smooth. Add to the puréed tomatoes. Stir in the lemon juice and rind, sherry and brown sugar. Season with the salt, pepper and Tabasco sauce. Refrigerate until well chilled.

**TO SERVE:** Spoon into bowls and garnish with the cucumber and parsley.

Serves 6–8

# Chilled cucumber and avocado soup

**MAKE AHEAD:** This soup can be made up to 2 days ahead, but if so, refrigerate until ready to serve.

2 English cucumbers, peeled
6 avocados, peeled and pips removed
1 small red onion
500 ml vegetable stock (15 ml stock
    powder mixed with 500 ml
    boiling water)
250 ml full-cream Greek-style yoghurt
15 ml salt crystals
2 ml curry powder
2 ml freshly ground black pepper
30 ml fresh lemon juice
sliced red onion, garlic flowers and
    freshly ground black pepper,
    for serving

Purée the cucumbers, avocados and onion in a food processor (fitted with the metal blade) until smooth. Add the remaining ingredients except the garnish, and blend thoroughly. Transfer to a large bowl and refrigerate.

**TO SERVE:** Spoon into bowls, and garnish with the onion, garlic flowers and pepper. Serve ice cold.

Serves 6

**CHEF'S NOTE:** Place the avocado pips in the soup to prevent discolouration and remove prior to serving.

# Summer fish salad

**MAKE AHEAD:** Make the dressing 1 day ahead and refrigerate until ready to serve.

1.5 kg monkfish or kingklip, skinned
    and filleted
30 ml olive oil
250 ml dry white wine
1 bay leaf
1 onion, chopped
3 sprigs parsley
3 celery stalks, chopped
5 ml salt
2 ml freshly ground black pepper
1 x 410 g can butter beans, drained
250 ml black olives, drained
3 celery stalks, sliced
1 red onion, thinly sliced
200 g cherry tomatoes, halved
30 g fresh watercress
30 g fresh rocket

DRESSING
juice of 1 lemon
125 ml cooking oil
125 ml olive oil
5 ml crushed garlic
10 ml Dijon mustard
10 ml chopped fresh dill
10 ml white sugar
7 ml salt crystals
2 ml freshly ground black pepper
30 ml chopped fresh parsley

Preheat the oven to 180 °C.

Coat a roasting pan with cooking spray. Place the fillets in the prepared pan and pour over the olive oil and wine. Add the bay leaf, onion, parsley, chopped celery, salt and pepper. Cover with foil and bake for 1 hour, or until cooked. Remove the fish from the oven and, using a slotted spoon, transfer to a cutting board. Allow to cool, then cut into chunks and spoon into a bowl.

Add the remaining ingredients and refrigerate until ready to serve.

**TO MAKE THE DRESSING:** Blend all the ingredients in the bowl of a food processor (fitted with the metal blade) and refrigerate until ready to use.

**TO SERVE:** Transfer the salad to a platter and spoon the dressing over.

Serves 6

# Honey-roasted baby chickens

**MAKE AHEAD:** Make the stuffing and glaze 1 day ahead, then refrigerate until ready to use.

6 baby chickens, trimmed

10 ml salt crystals

5 ml freshly ground black pepper

sprigs fresh lemon thyme, for serving

2 lemons cut into wedges, for serving

STUFFING

500 ml cooked brown rice

3 carrots, peeled and chopped

6 celery stalks, chopped

4 spring onions, thinly sliced

1 green pepper, seeded and
   chopped

250 ml fresh sprouts

30 ml cooking oil

5 ml crushed garlic

10 ml fresh ginger, crushed

5 ml salt crystals

2 ml freshly ground black pepper

GLAZE

100 ml honey

100 ml soy sauce

100 ml cooking oil

Preheat the oven to 200 °C. Coat a roasting pan with cooking spray and set aside.

Season the chickens with the salt and pepper. Spoon in the stuffing and truss neatly. Transfer the chickens to the prepared pan, cover with foil and roast for 1 hour. Remove from the oven, discard the foil and coat the chickens with the glaze. Return to the oven and roast for 30 minutes until golden and tender.

**TO MAKE THE STUFFING:** Combine all the ingredients in a bowl and refrigerate until ready to use.

**TO MAKE THE GLAZE:** Combine all the ingredients in a small bowl and set aside until ready to use.

**TO SERVE:** Garnish with the lemon thyme and lemon wedges, and serve with  the Mustard Potato Salad.

Serves 6

# Mustard potato salad

700 g new potatoes, unpeeled

2 sprigs fresh rosemary

80 ml dry white wine

1 red onion, chopped

5 ml salt crystals

250 ml mayonnaise

15 ml Dijon mustard

15 ml wholegrain mustard

2 hard-boiled eggs, quartered

30 ml chopped fresh Italian parsley

Boil the potatoes and rosemary in a large, heavy-based saucepan of salted boiling water until tender. Drain, cut in half and transfer to a mixing bowl. While still hot, pour over the wine. Add the remaining ingredients and mix thoroughly.

**TO SERVE:** Transfer to a platter and serve.

Serves 6

**CHEF'S NOTE:** Potato salad must never be refrigerated because the potatoes become rubbery when cold.

# Rhubarb and strawberry pudding with cinnamon mascarpone

**MAKE AHEAD:** Make the pudding and the mascarpone 1 day ahead and refrigerate until ready to serve.

125 ml red wine

220 g castor sugar

1 stick cinnamon

500 g rhubarb, stringy fibres
    removed, cut into 4-cm pieces

500 g strawberries, hulled


CINNAMON MASCARPONE

250 g mascarpone

60 g castor sugar

5 ml ground cinnamon

Combine the wine, castor sugar and cinnamon in a large, heavy-based saucepan over low heat until the sugar dissolves. Bring to the boil. Add the rhubarb, cover and simmer for 10 minutes, or until tender. Add the strawberries and simmer for a further 3 minutes. Remove from the heat, discard the cinnamon stick and set aside to cool. Refrigerate until cold.

**TO MAKE THE CINNAMON MASCARPONE:** Combine all the ingredients in a small bowl and mix until smooth. Refrigerate until ready to serve.

**TO SERVE:** Serve the pudding with the cinnamon mascarpone on the side.

Serves 6

# Chocolate-orange tarts

**MAKE AHEAD:** The pastry cases can be made ahead of time and stored in an airtight container.

## PASTRY
250 g cake flour

1 ml salt

65 g icing sugar

150 g butter or margarine

1 jumbo egg white, for brushing

## FILLING
250 ml freshly squeezed orange juice, strained

30 ml orange jelly powder

grated rind of 1 orange

400 g good-quality dark chocolate

300 g butter

3 jumbo eggs

50 g castor sugar

15 ml orange liqueur

icing sugar, for serving

Preheat the oven to 200 °C. Coat six 12-cm round, loose-based tart tins with cooking spray and set aside.

**TO MAKE THE PASTRY:** Sift the flour, salt and icing sugar into a chilled mixing bowl. Rub in the butter or margarine with your fingertips until the mixture resembles breadcrumbs. Knead the dough until smooth. Shape the pastry into a ball, wrap in clingfilm and refrigerate until ready to use.

Line the base and sides of the prepared tins with the pastry and refrigerate for 20 minutes. Prick the bases and bake blind for 10 minutes. Remove from the oven and brush the pastry shells with the egg white and set aside to cool.

**TO MAKE THE FILLING:** Heat the orange juice and jelly powder in a small, heavy-based saucepan and bring to the boil. Remove from the heat and set aside to cool. Stir in the orange rind. Place the tart tins on a baking sheet and pour in the cooled jelly. Refrigerate until set. Melt the chocolate in a heatproof bowl over simmering water and stir in the butter. Remove from the heat and set aside. Whisk the eggs and castor sugar in a food mixer until light and creamy in colour. Stir in the liqueur. Add the chocolate mixture to the egg mixture and spoon the filling onto the jelly. Refrigerate until ready to serve.

**TO SERVE:** Dust with the icing sugar.

Makes 6

This page: Make a splash with brightly coloured towels and cushions.

Opposite: For a colourful floral display, use different-coloured vases filled with bold flowers and greenery.

This page and opposite: Brightly
coloured, funky plastic containers,
crockery and glassware will create the
right mood at the poolside.

# Tea party

Ribbon tea sandwiches

Open tea sandwiches

Red velvet cupcakes

Date and coffee syrup cake

White chocolate cake with dark chocolate glaze

Ricotta and praline tart

# Ribbon tea sandwiches

white, brown and pumpernickel
     bread, sliced and crusts removed

EGG MAYONNAISE FILLING
3 hard-boiled eggs, mashed
200 g chunky cottage cheese
3 ml salt
1 ml freshly ground black pepper
5 ml prepared English mustard
50 ml mayonnaise

**TO MAKE THE FILLING:** Combine all the filling ingredients in a mixing bowl and refrigerate until ready to use.

Spread alternate slices of white, brown and pumpernickel bread with the filling, ensuring that the centre slice is spread on both sides. Stack the slices. Wrap the sandwiches in foil and refrigerate until ready to serve.

**TO SERVE:** Remove from the fridge, unwrap and, using a sharp knife, cut into fingers.

Serves 6

# Open tea sandwiches

ciabatta bread, sliced

CUCUMBER AND
WATERCRESS TOPPING
60 g butter
2 English cucumbers, peeled and
     thinly sliced
40 g fresh watercress
40 g fresh sprouts
3 ml salt crystals

Spread the bread with the butter and top with the cucumber, watercress and sprouts. Sprinkle with the salt, wrap in foil and refrigerate until ready to serve.

**TO SERVE:** Remove from the fridge, unwrap and serve.

ROAST BEEF, BLUE CHEESE AND
WALNUT TOPPING
60 g butter
250 g rare roast beef, sliced
60 g creamy blue cheese, crumbled
30 g walnuts, toasted and chopped

Spread the bread with the butter and top with the beef, cheese and walnuts. Wrap in foil and refrigerate until ready to serve.

**TO SERVE:** Remove from the fridge, unwrap and serve.

Serves 6

# Red velvet cupcakes

**MAKE AHEAD:** If you're pressed for time, make these cupcakes 1 day ahead and store in an airtight container.

200 g butter or margarine
220 g white sugar
250 ml buttermilk
15 ml white vinegar
10 ml vanilla essence
2 jumbo eggs
30 ml cocoa powder
30 ml red food colouring
350 g cake flour
7 ml bicarbonate of soda
1 ml salt

CREAM CHEESE ICING
60 g butter or margarine
180 g icing sugar
200 g smooth cream cheese
5 ml vanilla essence
sugared cake decorations, for serving

Preheat the oven to 180 °C. Line 2 x 12-cup muffin tins with paper casings and set aside.

Cream the butter or margarine and sugar in a food mixer until light and creamy in colour. Beat in the buttermilk, vinegar, vanilla, eggs, cocoa and food colouring. Sift the flour, bicarbonate of soda and salt into a mixing bowl and add to the buttermilk mixture. Mix thoroughly. Spoon the mixture into the prepared tins, filling each paper case three-quarters full. Bake for 20 minutes, or until a skewer inserted into the centre comes out clean. Turn out onto a wire rack to cool.

**TO MAKE THE ICING:** Cream the butter or margarine and icing sugar in a food processor (fitted with the plastic blade) until creamy. Add the cream cheese and vanilla and beat until smooth. Spread the icing over the cupcakes and decorate with sugared cake decorations.

Makes 15

# Date and coffee syrup cake

**MAKE AHEAD:** The cake can be made 1 day ahead and stored in an airtight container.

200 g pitted dates, chopped
50 ml Cognac or brandy
15 ml instant coffee granules
250 ml boiling water
250 g butter
440 g castor sugar
3 jumbo eggs
5 ml vanilla essence
150 g ground almonds
200 g self-raising flour
5 ml bicarbonate of soda
20 g cocoa powder
100 ml buttermilk
15 ml icing sugar, for dusting

COFFEE SYRUP
180 g castor sugar
10 ml instant coffee granules
100 ml water

Preheat the oven to 190 °C. Coat a 21 x 11 cm Bundt tin with cooking spray and set aside.

Soak the dates in the Cognac in a small bowl and set aside until ready to use. Dissolve the coffee in the boiling water and set aside to cool. Cream the butter and castor sugar in a food mixer until light and creamy in colour. Add the eggs one at a time, beating thoroughly after each addition. Mix in the remaining ingredients, including the soaked dates and coffee. Spoon the batter into the prepared tin and bake for 50 minutes, or until a skewer inserted into the centre comes out clean. Remove from the oven and leave to cool in the tin for 15 minutes. Turn out onto a wire rack with a plate underneath. Prick the top of the cake with a skewer and pour the Coffee Syrup over the cake. Set aside to cool before dusting with icing sugar.

**TO MAKE THE SYRUP:** Heat all the ingredients in a small, heavy-based saucepan, stirring until the sugar has dissolved. Bring to the boil and pour over the cake.

# White chocolate cake
# with dark chocolate glaze

**MAKE AHEAD:** Make the cake 1 day ahead and store in an airtight container.

150 g good-quality white chocolate

200 g self-raising flour

5 ml baking powder

175 g castor sugar

85 g butter or margarine

2 jumbo eggs

50 ml milk

5 ml vanilla essence

DARK CHOCOLATE GLAZE

100 g good-quality dark chocolate

40 g butter or margarine

15 ml honey

Preheat the oven to 180 °C. Coat a 20-cm round, loose-based cake tin with cooking spray and set aside.

Melt the chocolate in a heatproof bowl over simmering water. Remove from the heat and spoon into the bowl of a food processor (fitted with the plastic blade). Add the remaining ingredients and mix thoroughly. Spoon the batter into the prepared tin and bake for 35 minutes, or until a skewer inserted into the centre comes out clean. Remove from the oven and leave to cool in the tin for 10 minutes. Turn out onto a wire rack with a plate underneath and leave to cool. Pour the dark chocolate glaze over the cake.

**TO MAKE THE GLAZE:** Mix together the chocolate, butter and honey in a small, heavy-based saucepan. Bring to the boil, remove from the heat and pour over the cake.

# Ricotta and praline tart

PASTRY
225 g cake flour
2.5 ml salt
10 ml castor sugar
175 g butter or margarine
1 jumbo egg yolk
10 ml cold water

PRALINE
160 g castor sugar
150 ml water
3 ml cream of tartar
100 g whole blanched almonds,
    toasted
100 g pecan nuts, toasted

FILLING
350 g ricotta cheese, drained and
    crumbled
100 ml fresh cream
2 jumbo eggs
60 g castor sugar
10 ml grated orange rind

Coat a 24-cm round, loose-based tart tin with cooking spray and set aside.

**TO MAKE THE PASTRY:** Sift the flour and salt into a large, chilled mixing bowl and stir in the castor sugar. Cut the butter or margarine into the flour with a palette knife, then rub in lightly with your fingertips until the mixture resembles breadcrumbs. Make a well in the centre and pour in the egg yolk and water. Stir the liquid into the mixture with a chilled palette knife. Shape the pastry into a ball, turn out onto a lightly floured surface and knead until smooth. Wrap the pastry in clingfilm and refrigerate for 30 minutes, or until ready to use. Line the base and sides of the prepared tart tin with the pastry. Bake blind at 200 °C for 15 minutes and set aside to cool.

**TO MAKE THE PRALINE:** Line a baking sheet with baking paper. Coat the paper with cooking spray and set aside. Combine the castor sugar and water in a small, heavy-based saucepan, heat and stir until the sugar dissolves. Bring to the boil, add the cream of tartar and boil without stirring until golden in colour. Remove from the heat, add the nuts and stir. Spoon onto the prepared sheet and set aside to cool. Break the praline into pieces, grind coarsely in a food processor (fitted with the metal blade) and set aside until ready to use.

**TO MAKE THE FILLING:** Combine all the ingredients in the bowl of a food processor (fitted with the plastic blade) and mix thoroughly. Transfer to a mixing bowl and set aside until ready to use. Mix two-thirds of the praline into the ricotta mixture and spoon into the prepared pastry case. Bake at 180 °C for 30 minutes or until firm to the touch. Remove from the oven and set aside to cool. Sprinkle the remaining praline over the tart.

This page and opposite: Nothing says 'tea party' as well as porcelain, silver, a decorative tablecloth and an abundance of roses to re-create the spirit of a beautiful English garden.

This page and opposite: Cushions banded together with decorative ribbon, and chairs and folded napkins topped with roses capture the the mood.

# Retro party

French onion soup

Cheese soufflé

Caesar salad

Roast duck with orange sauce

Brown sugar carrots

Self-saucing mini chocolate puddings with fruit compote

# French onion soup

60 g butter
6 large onions, thinly sliced
10 ml crushed garlic
1.5 litres beef stock (30 ml stock powder mixed with
    1.5 litres boiling water)
5 ml salt
2 ml freshly ground black pepper
5 ml white sugar
30 ml brandy

CROUTONS
1 long French loaf, sliced and toasted
100 g Gruyère cheese, grated

Heat the butter in a large, heavy-based saucepan and sauté the onions and garlic. Cover and simmer for 20 minutes or until the onions are tender and golden in colour. Add the stock, salt, pepper and sugar and bring to the boil. Simmer for a further 40 minutes. Remove from the heat and stir in the brandy.

**TO MAKE THE CROUTONS:** Preheat the oven to 200 °C. Coat a baking sheet with cooking spray. Place the toast on the prepared sheet and top with the cheese. Bake for 5 minutes, or until the cheese has melted.

**TO SERVE:** Pour the soup into bowls, top with the croutons and serve hot.

Serves 6

# Cheese soufflé

10 ml butter, for greasing

20 ml grated Parmesan cheese,
    for coating

120 g butter

60 g cake flour

500 ml milk

8 jumbo eggs, separated

140 g Parmesan cheese, grated

100 g Gruyère cheese, grated

5 ml salt

2 ml cayenne pepper

2 ml mustard powder

Preheat the oven to 200 °C.

Grease six 10-cm diameter soufflé dishes with the butter. Coat with the 20 ml cheese, place on a baking sheet and set aside.

Melt the butter in a heavy-based saucepan and add the flour. Cook, stirring continuously, for 1 minute. Remove from the heat and stir in the milk. Return to medium heat, stirring continuously until the mixture boils and thickens. Remove the saucepan from the heat. Beat the egg yolks in a mixing bowl, and stir into the milk mixture. Return the saucepan to the heat and bring to the boil. Add the cheeses, salt, cayenne pepper and mustard powder then remove the saucepan from the heat. Using an electric beater, whisk the egg whites until stiff peaks form and fold into the cheese mixture using a metal spoon. Spoon the cheese mixture into the prepared dishes and bake for 20 minutes, or until puffed and golden. Serve immediately.

Serves 6

**CHEF'S NOTE:** Ensure the bowl and beaters are completely clean when beating the egg whites. Any egg yolk or egg shell will prevent the egg whites from stiffening.

# Caesar salad

2 heads cos lettuce, outer leaves
    removed
8 anchovy fillets, drained and
    chopped
60 g Parmesan cheese, sliced
250 ml readymade croutons

DRESSING
50 ml olive oil
50 ml cooking oil
5 ml crushed garlic
30 ml fresh lemon juice
10 ml Worcestershire sauce
5 ml mustard powder
3 ml salt
1 ml freshly ground black pepper
1 jumbo egg

Arrange the lettuce and anchovies on a serving platter and refrigerate until ready to use.

**TO MAKE THE DRESSING:** Blend all the ingredients in the bowl of a food processor (fitted with the metal blade) and refrigerate until ready to use.

**TO SERVE:** Spoon the dressing over the salad. Arrange the slices of cheese over the salad, sprinkle the croutons over and serve.

Serves 6

# Roast duck with orange sauce

2 ducks, trimmed

5 ml salt crystals

2 ml white pepper

5 ml chicken stock powder

1 onion, halved

50 ml chopped fresh parsley

1 litre water, to prevent dripping fat
    from smoking

fresh watercress, for serving

ORANGE SAUCE

rind of 2 oranges, thinly sliced

500 ml freshly squeezed orange juice

45 ml marmalade

30 ml fresh lemon juice

250 ml water

5 ml chicken stock powder

50 ml Van Der Hum® liqueur

30 ml cornflour mixed to a paste with
    30 ml cold water

Preheat the oven to 190 °C. Coat a rack and a roasting pan with cooking spray and set aside.

Clean the ducks, then season with the salt, pepper and stock powder. Place the onion and parsley into the cavities and truss neatly. Pour the water into the roasting pan and place the ducks onto the prepared rack. Roast, uncovered, for 2 hours, turning after 1 hour. Remove from the oven and place in the warming drawer for 15 minutes before portioning into quarters.

**TO MAKE THE SAUCE:** Pour the roasting liquid out of the roasting pan and discard, but retain the brown bits at the bottom of the pan. Add all the sauce ingredients to the roasting pan (including the brown bits) and stir. Bring all to the boil, cover and simmer for 20 minutes. Remove the roasting pan from the heat and keep the sauce warm until ready to use.

**TO SERVE:** Transfer the duck quarters to a serving platter, spoon the sauce over and serve with the Brown Sugar Carrots and watercress on the side.

Serves 6

# Brown sugar carrots

24 baby carrots, peeled

50 g butter

30 ml caramel brown sugar

15 ml honey

Bring the carrots to the boil in a large, heavy-based saucepan and boil for 4 minutes. Drain and refresh in cold water. Melt the butter in a large, heavy-based saucepan and add the sugar and honey. Add the carrots and toss until coated and reheated.

**TO SERVE:** Transfer to a serving platter.

Serves 6

# Self-saucing mini chocolate puddings with fruit compote

**MAKE AHEAD:** These puddings can be made up to 5 days ahead and frozen until ready to use. The compote can be made up to 2 days ahead and refrigerated until ready to serve.

150 g good-quality dark chocolate
150 g butter
3 jumbo eggs
3 jumbo egg yolks
90 g castor sugar
75 g cake flour
icing sugar, for serving

FRUIT COMPOTE
1 stick cinnamon
1 vanilla pod, split
2 whole cloves
6 coffee beans
125 g dried figs, halved
100 g dried pears, halved
50 g dried apple rings
250 ml sweet dessert wine
125 ml apple juice
1 firm pear, peeled, cored and sliced
1 firm green apple, peeled, cored
    and sliced

Preheat the oven to 220 °C. Coat six 10-cm dariole moulds with cooking spray, place on a baking tray and set aside.

Melt the chocolate and butter in a heatproof bowl over simmering water, stirring occasionally. Remove from the heat and set aside to cool. Beat the eggs, egg yolks and castor sugar together in a bowl until thick and pale in colour, then fold in the flour. Add the chocolate mixture and mix. Spoon the mixture into the prepared moulds, cover with clingfilm and freeze for 2 hours, or up to 5 days. Remove from the freezer and bake for 15 minutes or until the cake is firm around the edges and starts to come away from the sides of the moulds. Remove from the oven, run a palette knife around the edges of the moulds and invert onto individual serving plates.

**TO MAKE THE COMPOTE:** Combine the cinnamon stick, vanilla pod, cloves, coffee beans and dried fruit in a large, heavy-based saucepan. Add the wine and juice and bring to the boil. Cover and simmer for 15 minutes. Add the fresh pear and apple and cook until tender. Remove the saucepan from the heat, discard the vanilla pod, cinnamon stick and coffee beans, and set aside to cool. Spoon into a serving bowl.

**TO SERVE:** Dust the hot puddings with the icing sugar and serve immediately with the fruit compote on the side.

Makes 6

**This page:** Bunches of red tulips and tea lights in decorative candleholders complement this chic and sophisticated setting.

**Opposite:** Beautiful tableware is the foundation of any table setting.

**Above left:** Add a quirky element to give the room a lighthearted twist.

**Above right:** Tall vases filled with red tulips form the focal point of this setting.

**Opposite:** A simple, stylised tray set with coffee cups rounds off the meal.

# Festive celebration

Cold butternut and carrot soup

Cheese puffs

Smoked salmon with mustard-honey dressing

Festive turkey

Slow-roasted lamb shanks

Wasabi mash

Roasted balsamic asparagus

Pink peppercorn meringue with granadilla curd

Upside-down caramel plum cake

# Cold butternut and carrot soup

**MAKE AHEAD:** This soup can be made and refrigerated up to 2 days ahead.

30 ml olive oil

1 onion, sliced

1 kg butternut, peeled and cubed

350 g carrots, peeled and grated

2 litres vegetable stock (20 ml stock
   powder mixed with 2 litres
   boiling water)

7 ml salt crystals

1 ml white pepper

1 ml ground nutmeg

1 stick cinnamon

250 ml fresh cream

50 ml chopped fresh chives, for
   serving

Heat the olive oil in a heavy-based saucepan and sauté the onion until tender. Add the butternut and carrots, stirring frequently. Pour in the heated stock, salt, pepper, nutmeg and cinnamon stick, cover and simmer for 30 minutes, or until the vegetables are tender. Discard the cinnamon stick and purée the soup in a food processor (fitted with the metal blade) until smooth. Transfer to a mixing bowl, stir in the cream and refrigerate until ready to serve.

**TO SERVE:** Remove from the fridge, transfer to soup bowls and serve topped with the Cheese Puffs and chives.

Serves 6

# Cheese puffs

70 g cake flour

50 g butter or margarine

1 ml salt

125 ml water

2 jumbo eggs, beaten

50 g grated Parmesan cheese

**CHEF'S NOTE:** Sprinkle the baking sheet with water prior to baking. This creates steam and promotes the rising process.

Preheat the oven to 200 °C. Coat a baking sheet with cooking spray and set aside.

Sift the flour into a mixing bowl. Place the butter or margarine, salt and water into a small, heavy-based saucepan and bring to the boil. Stir continually with a wooden spoon. Remove the saucepan from the heat and spoon in the flour. Beat until smooth. Return the saucepan to the heat and beat for 1–2 minutes, or until the mixture forms a smooth ball. Remove the saucepan from the heat and leave to cool for 3 minutes. Beat in the eggs, a little at a time, with a wooden spoon. Beat in the cheese. Drop spoonfuls of the mixture onto the prepared sheet and bake for 20 minutes, or until a skewer inserted into the centre comes out clean. Remove from the oven and turn out onto a wire rack to cool.

Makes 12

# Smoked salmon with mustard-honey dressing

**MAKE AHEAD:** The dressing can be made and refrigerated up to 1 day ahead.

500 g smoked salmon or smoked
    salmon trout, cut into 2.5-cm strips
1 English cucumber, julienned
1 yellow pepper, seeded and julienned
4 spring onions, sliced
50 g fresh salad leaves

MUSTARD-HONEY DRESSING
200 ml buttermilk
30 ml Dijon mustard
15 ml honey
30 ml chopped fresh Italian parsley
1 ml white pepper

Arrange the salmon and remaining ingredients on individual serving plates and refrigerate until ready to serve.

**TO MAKE THE DRESSING:** Blend all the ingredients in a food processor (fitted with the plastic blade). Refrigerate until ready to use.

**TO SERVE:** Spoon the dressing over the salmon and serve.

Serves 6

# Festive turkey

1 whole turkey, trimmed (note the
    weight)
2 onions, sliced
4 carrots, peeled and sliced
4 celery stalks
50 ml fresh parsley
10 ml crushed garlic
30 ml soy sauce
10 ml salt
5 ml freshly ground black pepper
5 ml ground ginger
1.5 litres chicken stock (30 ml stock
    powder mixed with 1.5 litres
    boiling water)
fresh Italian parsley, for serving
cranberry jelly, for serving

GRAVY
reserved pan juices
50 ml white wine mixed to a paste
    with 30 ml gravy powder

Preheat the oven to 190 °C.

Coat a deep roasting pan with cooking spray. Clean the turkey and transfer
to the prepared pan. Add the onions, carrots, celery and parsley to the pan.
Rub the garlic, soy sauce, salt, pepper and ginger into the skin and cavity
of the turkey. Pour over the heated stock and cover the turkey with baking
paper. Place in the oven and roast, basting occasionally, for about 3 hours, or
for 60 minutes per 1 kg of the weight of the turkey. Turn the turkey every hour
and remove the baking paper for the final 30 minutes. Remove from the oven.

**TO MAKE THE GRAVY:** Strain the pan juices from the roasting pan into a
small, heavy-based saucepan. Add the white wine paste to the pan juices and
stir until thickened. Keep warm until ready to use.

**TO SERVE:** Transfer the turkey to a serving platter and garnish with the
Italian parsley. Serve with the gravy and cranberry jelly on the side.

Serves 6

# Slow-roasted lamb shanks

**MAKE AHEAD:** Lamb shanks can be made 1 day ahead and refrigerated until ready to reheat at 180 °C for 20 minutes.

6 lamb shanks, 19 cm in length

3 red onions, quartered

3 fresh bay leaves

5 ml crushed garlic

10 ml salt crystals

5 ml ground cumin

5 ml ground coriander

5 ml ground ginger

250 ml red wine

250 ml freshly squeezed orange juice

1 x 410 g can whole peeled
   tomatoes, chopped

500 ml meat stock (20 ml stock
   powder mixed with 500 ml
   boiling water)

Preheat the oven to 190 °C.

Coat a casserole dish with cooking spray. Transfer the shanks to the prepared dish and add the remaining ingredients. Cover and roast for 4 hours, or until the meat is tender. Remove from the oven and keep warm in the warming drawer until ready to serve.

**TO SERVE:** Transfer to a serving platter, spoon over the pan juices and serve with the Wasabi Mash and the Roasted Balsamic Asparagus.

Serves 6

# Wasabi mash

1 kg potatoes, peeled and quartered
50 g butter
5 ml salt
10 ml wasabi paste

Cook the potatoes in a large, heavy-based saucepan of boiling salted water until tender. Drain the potatoes, return to the saucepan and mix in the butter, salt and the wasabi paste. Mash until smooth.

Serves 6

# Roasted balsamic asparagus

1 kg fresh green asparagus
50 ml olive oil
5 ml crushed garlic
5 ml salt crystals
2 ml freshly ground black pepper
30 ml balsamic vinegar, for serving

Preheat the oven to 220 °C. Coat a large roasting pan with cooking spray and set aside.

Cut off the ends of the asparagus, rinse and drain. Transfer the asparagus to the prepared pan and sprinkle over the oil, garlic, salt and pepper. Roast for 10–15 minutes, or until cooked. Remove from the oven and keep warm until ready to serve.

**TO SERVE:** Transfer to a serving platter, sprinkle with the balsamic vinegar and serve.

Serves 6

# Pink peppercorn meringue with granadilla curd

4 jumbo egg whites

2 ml salt

300 g castor sugar

5 ml white vinegar

5 ml vanilla essence

15 ml cornflour

15 ml pink peppercorns, crushed

500 g fresh strawberries, halved

icing sugar, for serving

GRANADILLA CURD

250 ml fresh cream, whipped

125 ml lemon curd

1 x 110 g can granadilla pulp

**CHEF'S NOTE:** For a smooth meringue, rub a little of the pre-baked mixture between two fingers. If any of the sugar granules are visible, beat a little longer.

Preheat the oven to 200 °C. Line a baking sheet with baking paper and set aside.

Using an electric mixer, beat the egg whites and salt until soft peaks begin to form. Gradually add the castor sugar, beating until stiff peaks begin to form once more. Add the vinegar, vanilla, cornflour and peppercorns. Spoon the meringue onto the prepared sheet and shape into a circle, 20 cm in diameter. Using a metal spoon, shape the edges to create a cavity.

Reduce the oven temperature to 120 °C and bake for 1 hour. Remove from the oven and set aside to cool.

**TO MAKE THE GRANADILLA CURD:** Mix together all the ingredients in a small bowl. Refrigerate until ready to use.

**TO SERVE:** Spoon the granadilla curd into the cavity in the meringue, top with the fresh strawberries and dust with the icing sugar.

Serves 6

# Upside-down caramel plum cake

100 g butter or margarine
200 g castor sugar
2 jumbo eggs
200 g self-raising flour
5 ml ground cinnamon
2 ml ground nutmeg
2 ml salt
1 ripe banana, mashed
30 ml fresh cream

TOPPING
60 g butter
160 g golden brown sugar
30 ml golden syrup
8 ripe plums, sliced

Preheat the oven to 180 °C. Coat a 24-cm round, loose-based cake tin with cooking spray and set aside.

**TO MAKE THE TOPPING:** Melt the butter in a small, heavy-based saucepan, then add the sugar and syrup and stir. Bring to the boil and cook for 3 minutes. Remove from the heat and pour the mixture into the prepared tin. Arrange the plum slices, skin side down, in concentric circles in the topping mixture.

**TO MAKE THE CAKE:** Cream the butter or margarine and castor sugar in the bowl of a food mixer until light and creamy in colour. Mix in the eggs. Sift the flour, spices and salt into a bowl and add, alternately with the banana and cream, to the butter mixture. Spoon the batter into the prepared tin over the topping and bake for 45 minutes, or until a skewer inserted into the centre comes out clean. Remove from the oven and leave to cool in the tin for 20 minutes. Run a sharp knife around the edge of the tin and invert the cake onto a serving plate.

**TO SERVE:** Serve warm.

Serves 6

**This page and opposite:** Glamorous crystal and ornate elements add to the air of festivity in this setting.

**This page and opposite:** Varying shades of pink and purple flowers in the shape

of topiary balls, combined with chunky candles set on a dark wooden table,

enhance this festive occasion.

# Buffet party

Prawn kebabs

Chicken, almond and orange salad

Thai cucumber pickle

Veal osso bucco

Broccoli with walnut dressing

Biscuit-layered pineapple mousse

Rose-scented fruit salad

White chocolate bark

# Prawn kebabs

24 king prawns, cleaned and deveined
10 ml crushed garlic
75 ml fresh lemon juice
10 ml salt crystals
75 ml readymade peanut sauce
12 small wooden skewers, soaked in water for 2 hours to prevent burning
lime wedges, for serving

Preheat the oven to 230 °C. Line a baking sheet with baking paper and
set aside.

Season the prawns with the garlic, lemon juice, salt and peanut sauce. Thread
the prawns onto the prepared skewers and place on the baking sheet. Bake
for 6 minutes per side, or until cooked. Remove from the oven.

**TO SERVE:** Arrange on a serving platter, top with the lime wedges, then
serve immediately.

Serves 12

# Chicken, almond and orange salad

100 g fresh mixed salad leaves, e.g.
    baby spinach, watercress
    and rocket
2 cooked chickens, skinned and
    filleted, cut into bite-sized pieces
2 oranges, peeled and thinly sliced
40 g pumpkin seeds, toasted
100 g whole skinned almonds,
    toasted

DRESSING
100 ml olive oil
50 ml red wine vinegar
5 ml wholegrain mustard
2 ml salt
1 ml freshly ground black pepper

Place the salad leaves, chicken and the oranges on a serving platter. Sprinkle the pumpkin seeds and almonds over. Cover with clingfilm and refrigerate until ready to use.

**TO MAKE THE DRESSING:** Blend all the ingredients in the bowl of a food processor (fitted with the metal blade) and refrigerate until ready to use.

**TO SERVE:** Spoon the dressing over the salad and serve.

Serves 12

# Thai cucumber pickle

**MAKE AHEAD:** The pickle can be made and refrigerated up to 3 days ahead.

3 English cucumbers, sliced
1 red onion, sliced
1 red chilli, seeded and sliced
500 ml rice vinegar
60 ml white sugar
5 ml salt
5 ml black peppercorns
10 ml mustard seeds
25 ml chopped fresh coriander

Combine all the ingredients in a large mixing bowl and refrigerate until ready to serve.

Serves 12

# Veal osso bucco

**MAKE AHEAD:** This dish can be made up to 2 days ahead. Refrigerate, then reheat at 180 °C.

12 slices shin of veal, 2.5 cm thick
50 ml cooking oil
2 onions, sliced
3 carrots, peeled and sliced
6 celery stalks, sliced
3 fresh bay leaves
5 ml crushed garlic
10 ml salt crystals
2 ml freshly ground black pepper
juice and rind of 1 lemon
1 x 115 g can tomato paste
1 x 410 g can whole peeled
    tomatoes, chopped
125 ml white wine
500 ml meat stock (30 ml stock
    powder mixed with 500 ml
    boiling water)
sprigs fresh parsley, for serving

Preheat the oven to 180 °C.

Brown the meat in the heated cooking oil in a large, heavy-based casserole dish. Add the onions, carrots and celery and sauté. Add the remaining ingredients, except the parsley. Cover with a lid and roast for 4 hours, or until the meat is tender. Remove from the oven and keep warm in the warming drawer until ready to serve.

**TO SERVE:** Transfer to a serving dish and garnish with the fresh parsley and serve with the Broccoli with Walnut Dressing.

Serves 12

# Broccoli with walnut dressing

800 g fresh broccoli spears

100 g whole walnuts

50 ml olive oil

2 ml salt

1 ml freshly ground black pepper

Steam the broccoli for 6 minutes, or until tender. Dry-fry the walnuts in a small, heavy-based frying pan for 3 minutes. Add the olive oil and fry for a further 2 minutes. Remove from the heat and pour over the broccoli. Season with the salt and pepper.

**TO SERVE:** Transfer to a serving platter.

Serves 12

# Biscuit-layered pineapple mousse

**MAKE AHEAD:** This dessert can be made and refrigerated 1 day ahead.

2 x 200 g packets Tennis® biscuits

100 g butter or margarine

1 x 840 g can pineapple pieces,
    drained (juice reserved)

2 x 80 g packets pineapple or
    lemon jelly

2 x 380 g cans evaporated milk,
    refrigerated overnight

PINEAPPLE WAFERS

200 g white sugar

250 ml boiling water

6 very thin slices pineapple, halved

Coat 12 glasses with cooking spray and set aside.

Crush the biscuits finely in a food processor (fitted with the metal blade) and spoon into a small mixing bowl. Melt the butter or margarine in a small bowl in the microwave at 100% power for 1 minute and combine with the crumbs. Spoon a layer of the crumb mixture onto the base of 12 glasses and set aside. (Reserve a little of the crumb mixture.) Bring the pineapple juice and the jelly to the boil in a small, heavy-based saucepan. Remove from the heat and set aside to cool. Beat the evaporated milk in the bowl of a food mixer until thick and creamy. Pour in the jelly mixture and the pineapple pieces and beat thoroughly. Spoon the pineapple mousse into the glasses, top with the remaining crumb mixture and refrigerate.

**TO MAKE THE PINEAPPLE WAFERS:** Pour the sugar and water into a heavy-based saucepan. Bring to the boil until the sugar dissolves, but do not stir. Dip the pineapple slices in the syrup and arrange on a non-stick baking tray. Bake at 120 °C for 45–60 minutes. Leave to cool. The slices will crisp on standing.

**TO SERVE:** Decorate with the pineapple wafers.

Serves 12

# Rose-scented fruit salad

**MAKE AHEAD:** Make the syrup 1 day ahead and refrigerate.

1 kg ripe lychees, peeled

1.5 kg seedless watermelon, rind
    removed, and cubed

1 ripe pineapple, peeled, cored
    and cubed

6 ripe nectarines, quartered
    and stoned

6 ripe plums, quartered and stoned

250 g ripe raspberries

rose petals and fresh mint, for serving

SUGAR SYRUP

250 ml water

150 g castor sugar

30 ml fresh lemon juice

1 vanilla pod, split

10 ml rosewater

Place the prepared fruit in a bowl and refrigerate until ready to serve.

**TO MAKE THE SYRUP:** Combine the water, castor sugar and lemon juice in a small, heavy-based saucepan. Scrape the seeds from the vanilla pod into the syrup mixture and bring to the boil. Remove from the heat and stir in the rosewater. Set aside to cool.

**TO SERVE:** Spoon into serving bowls and pour over the sugar syrup. Decorate with the rose petals and mint.

Serves 12

# White chocolate bark

**MAKE AHEAD:** Make the bark 1 day ahead and store in a cool place.

500 g good-quality white chocolate,
    broken into pieces

200 g walnuts, toasted and roughly
    chopped

150 g dried cranberries

Line a 33 x 22 cm lamington tin with baking paper and set aside.

Melt the chocolate in a heatproof bowl over simmering water. Remove from the heat and stir until smooth. Stir in the nuts and cranberries and pour the mixture into the prepared tin. Set aside to cool and break into shards.

Serves 12

**Right top:** Pine cones stacked in a glass bowl create a simple but striking table decoration.

**Right centre:** Instead of a conventional vase for these orchids, use what nature provides as a creative alternative.

**Right bottom:** Pack cutlery into rectangular boxes – it's functional and attractive.

**Opposite:** A combination of structured shapes puts the focus on the food and décor elements.

Opposite: Folded serviettes,
a Perspex box filled with glasses and
piled plates set the scene for an elegant,
outdoor buffet.

Right: Potted orchids planted in
a pebble-filled square glass vase.

# Midweek family dinner

Baked rigatoni and cheese

Curried banana meatballs

Green beans with French vinaigrette

Ginger crumble

Vanilla ice cream

Hot chocolate sauce

# Baked rigatoni and cheese

500 g rigatoni
5 ml salt crystals
120 g butter or margarine
120 g cake flour
1.25 litres milk
250 g Cheddar cheese, grated
1 ml cayenne pepper
1 ml mustard powder
120 g Cheddar cheese, grated

Preheat the oven to 190 °C. Coat a 24-cm round, springform tin with cooking spray and set aside.

Boil the pasta in a large, heavy-based saucepan of boiling water until *al dente*. Drain and transfer to the prepared tin. Sprinkle the salt over and set aside until ready to use. Melt the butter or margarine in a heavy-based saucepan and add the flour. Cook, stirring continuously, for 1 minute. Remove the saucepan from the heat and gradually whisk in the milk, stirring continually over medium heat until the mixture boils and thickens. Remove the saucepan from the heat and add the 250 g cheese, cayenne pepper and mustard powder and stir until the cheese has melted. Pour the sauce over the pasta and mix thoroughly. Sprinkle with the remaining cheese and bake for 30 minutes, or until golden in colour. Remove from the oven and leave to cool in the tin for 10 minutes.

**TO SERVE:** Transfer to a serving platter.

Serves 6

# Curried banana meatballs

**MAKE AHEAD:** Prepare this dish 1 day ahead and refrigerate until ready to bake.

2 onions, chopped
2 apples, cored and chopped
8 prunes, pitted and chopped
1 kg lean beef mince
7 ml salt crystals
2 ml freshly ground black pepper

CURRY BANANA SAUCE
30 ml cooking oil
3 onions, chopped
30 ml mild curry powder
30 ml cake flour
250 ml brown vinegar
500 ml water
100 ml smooth apricot jam
50 ml caramel brown sugar
2 fresh bay leaves
6 bananas, peeled and sliced

Preheat the oven to 180 °C. Coat an ovenproof casserole dish with cooking spray and set aside.

Combine all the ingredients in a bowl and shape into balls. Transfer the meatballs to the prepared dish and set aside until ready to use.

**TO MAKE THE SAUCE:** Heat the cooking oil in a heavy-based saucepan and sauté the onions. Add the curry powder and flour and cook for 1 minute. Add the remaining ingredients, bring to the boil, cover and simmer for 10 minutes. Remove the saucepan from the heat and pour the sauce over the meatballs. Bake for 1½ hours, or until cooked.

**TO SERVE:** Serve with rice, chutney, a tomato and onion sambal, and the Green Beans with French Vinaigrette.

Serves 6

**CHEF'S NOTE:** Minced meat, whether raw or cooked, should only be kept in the fridge for up to 3 days. Purchase the mince on the day or pack into airtight containers and freeze for up to 3 months.

# Green beans with French vinaigrette

700 g green beans, trimmed and
    blanched
125 ml olive oil
30 ml white wine vinegar
10 ml Dijon mustard
30 ml fresh lemon juice
5 ml crushed garlic
5 ml salt crystals
2 ml freshly ground black pepper
fresh coriander, for serving

Combine all the ingredients except the coriander in a large, heavy-based saucepan. Bring to the boil and cook for 2 minutes. Remove the saucepan from the heat.

**TO SERVE:** Spoon the beans and vinaigrette onto a serving platter and top with the coriander.

Serves 6

# Ginger crumble

**MAKE AHEAD:** This dessert can be made 1 day ahead. Keep refrigerated, then reheat gently before serving.

2 x 200 g packets Ginger Nut® biscuits
100 g butter or margarine
1 x 410 g can mango slices in syrup
1 x 576 g can pitted lychees in syrup
1 x 425 g can pitted black cherries in syrup
fresh cream, whipped, for serving

GLAZE
350 ml reserved syrup (from mango slices, lychees and cherries)
30 ml custard powder
30 ml cherry liqueur

Preheat the oven to 180 °C. Coat 6 ovenproof ramekins with cooking spray and set aside.

Crush the biscuits finely in a food processor (fitted with the metal blade) and spoon into a small mixing bowl. Melt the butter or margarine in a small bowl in the microwave at 100% power for 1 minute, then combine with the crumbs and set aside.

Spoon the fruit into the prepared ramekins and pour over the glaze. Sprinkle the crumb mixture over the top and bake for 15 minutes. Remove from the oven and keep warm in the warming drawer.

**TO MAKE THE GLAZE:** Drain the fruit into a mixing bowl, reserving 350 ml of the combined syrups. Heat 300 ml of the syrup in a small, heavy-based saucepan and bring to the boil. Mix the custard powder to a paste with the remaining 50 ml syrup, stir into the heated syrup and boil for 1 minute. Remove the saucepan from the heat and stir in the liqueur.

**TO SERVE:** Top with the cream.

Serves 6

# Vanilla ice cream

**MAKE AHEAD:** The ice cream can be made up to 3 days ahead.

8 jumbo egg yolks
220 g castor sugar
750 ml fresh cream
250 ml milk
1 vanilla pod, split
Maraschino cherries, for serving

Coat a decorative mould with cooking spray and set aside.

Beat the egg yolks and castor sugar in a food mixer until light and creamy in colour. Heat the cream, milk and the seeds from the vanilla pod in a large, heavy-based saucepan and bring almost to the boil. Remove the saucepan from the heat and add to the egg mixture. Mix thoroughly and return to the saucepan. Stirring continually, heat over medium heat until the mixture coats the back of a wooden spoon. Do not boil. Transfer the mixture into an ice cream maker and churn for 20 minutes, or until smooth. Pour the ice cream into the prepared mould and freeze until ready to serve.

**TO SERVE:** Serve the ice cream in attractive bowls or parfait glasses, spoon the Hot Chocolate Sauce over and decorate with a cherry each.

Serves 6

# Hot chocolate sauce

500 ml fresh cream
100 g dark chocolate
100 g milk chocolate
100 g white chocolate
10 ml vanilla essence

Place all the ingredients (except the vanilla essence) in a heavy-based saucepan and cook over low heat, stirring continually with a wooden spoon until the chocolate has melted. Bring to the boil and simmer for 10 minutes. Remove the saucepan from the heat and stir in the vanilla. Keep warm until ready to serve.

Serves 6

This page and opposite: An assortment of Blue Delft bowls filled with balls, pomegranates and flowers.

This page and opposite: Blue Delft, white crockery, flowers and candles create an inviting, homely atmosphere.

# Red, white and green party

Italian crisp bread

Rocket and cherry tomato salad

Pappardelle with chicken and butternut ragu

Courgette, pea and artichoke risotto

Layered lemon mousse

Frangelico crème brûlée

# Italian crisp bread

1 x 10 g packet instant dry yeast
5 ml white sugar
25 ml lukewarm water
350 g white bread flour
5 ml salt
25 ml olive oil
200 ml lukewarm water
75 ml olive oil, for brushing
30 ml coarse salt
50 ml chopped fresh rosemary

**CHEF'S NOTE:** The crisp bread is best eaten warm from the oven but may be reheated (wrapped in foil) at 180 °C.

Preheat the oven to 230 °C. Coat a 39 x 26 cm baking sheet with olive oil and set aside.

Combine the yeast, sugar and 25 ml water in a bowl and mix to form a thin cream. Sift the flour and salt into a bowl. Make a well in the centre and pour in the yeast mixture, 25 ml oil and 200 ml water. Mix thoroughly. Turn the dough out onto a lightly floured surface and knead for 10 minutes. Place the dough in a bowl and refrigerate for 20 minutes. Remove from the fridge, divide the dough into 12 pieces and roll out thinly onto the lightly floured surface. Brush with the 75 ml oil and sprinkle with the salt and rosemary. Place onto the prepared sheet and bake for 6 minutes. Remove from the oven and turn out onto a wire rack to cool.

Serves 6

# Rocket and cherry tomato salad

**MAKE AHEAD:** Make the dressing for this starter 1 day ahead and refrigerate.

240 g rocket leaves
400 g cherry tomatoes
1 bunch spring onions, thinly sliced
2 avocados, peeled, pip removed
    and cubed

DRESSING
100 ml olive oil
40 ml white wine vinegar
30 ml honey
30 ml wholegrain mustard
2 ml salt
1 ml white pepper

Combine all the salad ingredients in a bowl and refrigerate.

**TO MAKE THE DRESSING:** Blend all the ingredients in the bowl of a food processor (fitted with the metal blade) and refrigerate until ready to use.

**TO SERVE:** Spoon the dressing over the salad and serve.

Serves 6

# Pappardelle with chicken and butternut ragu

400 g pappardelle

5 ml salt

45 ml olive oil

6 skinless chicken breast fillets, cut into pieces

2 onions, sliced

10 ml crushed garlic

6 celery stalks, sliced

500 g butternut, peeled and cubed

2 fresh bay leaves

2 ml freshly ground black pepper

125 ml white wine

250 ml chicken stock (10 ml stock powder mixed with 250 ml boiling water)

15 ml cornflour mixed to a paste with 15 ml cold water

100 g Parmesan cheese, grated, for serving

20 g fresh basil, for serving

Boil the pasta in a large, heavy-based saucepan of boiling water until *al dente*. Drain and sprinkle with the salt and set aside until ready to use. Heat the olive oil in a large, heavy-based frying pan and sauté the chicken until golden in colour. Remove from the pan and set aside until ready to use.

Using the same pan, sauté the onions, garlic, celery and butternut. Add the remaining ingredients, except the cheese and basil. Cover and simmer for 30 minutes, or until cooked and all the liquid has been absorbed. Remove from the heat and combine with the chicken.

**TO SERVE:** Spoon the pasta and the chicken mixture onto a serving platter, top with the cheese and basil and serve.

Serves 6

**CHEF'S NOTE:** If serving the Courgette, Pea and Artichoke Risotto as a main course in addition to the Pappardelle with Chicken and Butternut Ragu, the combined meal would serve 12.

# Courgette, pea and artichoke risotto

30 g butter

30 ml olive oil

2 red onions, chopped

10 ml crushed garlic

250 g Arborio rice

5 ml salt

50 ml white wine

1 litre vegetable stock (30 ml stock powder mixed with
    1 litre boiling water)

400 g courgettes (baby marrows), sliced

250 g frozen peas

1 x 400 g can artichoke hearts, drained and quartered

100 g Parmesan cheese, grated

50 g Parmesan cheese shavings, for serving

50 g fresh peas, for serving

Heat the butter and olive oil in a large, heavy-based saucepan and sauté the onions and garlic. Add the rice and salt and sauté for 2 minutes. Add the wine and heated stock. Cover and simmer for 30 minutes, or until nearly cooked. Add the courgettes, frozen peas and artichokes and simmer for a further 10 minutes, stirring frequently. Remove the saucepan from the heat and stir in the grated cheese.

**TO SERVE:** Spoon into bowls and top with the Parmesan shavings and peas.

Serves 6 (see chef's note on page 193)

# Layered lemon mousse

**MAKE AHEAD:** This dessert can be made and refrigerated up to 2 days ahead.

1 grapefruit, peeled and sliced,
    for serving
1 orange, peeled and sliced,
    for serving
Amaretti biscuits, for serving

LEMON CURD
175 g castor sugar
3 jumbo eggs, beaten
125 g butter
200 ml fresh lemon juice

LEMON MOUSSE
4 gelatine sheets
200 ml fresh lemon juice
150 g castor sugar
250 ml fresh cream, whipped

**TO MAKE THE CURD:** Combine all the ingredients in a heatproof bowl over a saucepan of simmering water and whisk until thick and glossy. Remove the bowl from the heat, set aside to cool and refrigerate until ready to use.

**TO MAKE THE MOUSSE:** Soak the gelatine sheets in a plate of cold water until soft and set aside until ready to use. Bring the lemon juice and castor sugar to the boil in a heavy-based saucepan, stirring until the sugar dissolves. Remove from the heat. Drain the excess water off the gelatine, stir the gelatine into the lemon mixture and refrigerate until almost set. Remove from the fridge and stir in the cream.

**TO ASSEMBLE:** Spoon the curd into a bowl and top with the mousse. Refrigerate until set.

**TO SERVE:** Decorate with the fruit and serve with the biscuits on the side.

Serves 6

# Frangelico® crème brûlée

**MAKE AHEAD:** Crème brûlée must be made at least 1 day ahead, but not longer than 2 days ahead.

850 ml fresh cream
8 jumbo egg yolks
100 g castor sugar
70 ml Frangelico® liqueur
60 ml castor sugar, for serving

Preheat the oven to 180 °C. Coat 6 small ovenproof ramekins with cooking spray, place in a roasting pan lined with 3 sheets of newspaper and set aside.

Heat the cream in a heavy-based saucepan until scalding point. Remove from the heat. Beat the egg yolks and castor sugar in a mixing bowl until pale and creamy in colour. Pour the cream into the egg mixture, whisking thoroughly. Stir in the liqueur. Pour the mixture into the prepared ramekins. Pour hot water into the roasting pan to reach halfway up the sides of the ramekins. Bake for 35 minutes, or until set. The custard should come away from the side of the ramekin but the centre should still be a bit wobbly. Remove from the oven and set aside to cool. Refrigerate overnight.

**TO SERVE:** Sprinkle 10 ml castor sugar evenly over the top of each custard and caramelise with a blowtorch or place the ramekins under the grill of a very hot oven. Serve immediately.

Serves 6

**CHEF'S NOTE:** Lining the baking tin with 3 sheets of newspaper acts as an insulator and prevents the custard from curdling.

This page and opposite: Bold-coloured glassware, rustic crockery, vegetables and grapes set the scene for a traditional, Italian-style function.

**Above left:** Create a sense of abundance with baskets overflowing with peppers and grapes.

**Right:** A folded napkin with an elegantly placed flower adds to the charm of an informal setting.

**Top:** A strategically placed, rustic
container filled with bright red flowers
catches the eye.

# Elements
## of the table

How you choose to set and decorate the table contributes to the overall
mood of any party. The following section includes some easy-to-do ideas that will transform
an everyday table into a festive one!

**Above:** Fill three cylindrical vases with broken sea shells and plant succulents in the centre of each vase. Use these as an unusual centrepiece on the table.

# Brunch

The setting for the brunch is on the deck of a beach house with the table set in shades of white, turquoise and blue to reflect the colours of the sea and sky. The tableware is anchored with glass vases filled with broken sea shells and succulents, creating a stylish centrepiece. Sea shells have also been used to make napkin rings – bringing the natural elements of the surroundings to the table top. This menu and table setting can be recreated on a home patio, adding glass vases filled with pebbles and sprigs of beach grass to replicate the carefree mood of a brunch at the seaside. Follow the path of the sun the day before and find a spot for the table with the right mix of shade and sun. Fill decanters with fruit juice to add a splash of colour. For deliciously scented hand towels, infuse fresh herbs such as mint and slices of lemon in boiling water in a heatproof bowl and soak rolled napkins in the infusion. Once cool, wring out the napkins and arrange them on a tray and offer them to the guests.

**Above:** Place cutlery in a cylindrical vase as an alternative to setting the table. More than one vase may be used.

# Spring lunch

There is nothing as pleasurable as being seated at a table basking in the warmth of a spring afternoon, enjoying good company. To set the mood for the spring lunch bunches of spring flowers are grouped in clear glass vases and the table is dressed with a crisp green tablecloth and special-occasion crockery, cutlery and glasses. When planning the menu make the most of the season's fresh ingredients. Open a chilled bottle of Champagne or sparkling wine to celebrate this joyful season. Bring a decorative touch to each place setting with patterned napkins and fold them in a functional way. Keep the centre arrangement low, so it won't block the lines of sight or prevent an easy flow of conversation. Clear glass vases, serving platters and dishes keep the setting simple and allow the focus to be on the brightly coloured flowers and delicious food. Plate the food in the kitchen in order to keep the table uncluttered and position the table close to the kitchen for ease in serving.

**Above:** Fill different sizes and shapes of glass vases with water. Bunch each type of flower together and place in the vases. Group them on the table as desired. Lower-positioned vases and shorter flowers can be used as a variation.

**Left:** Cut flowers very short, leaving a 1-cm stem. Centre a side plate onto a dinner plate, then arrange the cut flowers by tucking the stems under the edge of the side plate, creating a floral edge.

# Cocktail party

Take advantage of the surroundings and use them as a backdrop to the occasion. As the sun sets and the cityscape below begins to sparkle, the setting is illuminated with decorative lights strung overhead. Dramatic décor such as white-plumed ostrich feathers spot lit on stark, black platforms create a chic, minimalistic look for the cocktail party. Greet guests with an aperitif such as Champagne or fruity cocktails served in martini glasses to add a touch of glamour. Supplement with a self-serve bar that includes wine, water, juice and soft drinks, allowing one bottle of wine and one litre of water for every three guests. Serve mostly cold or room-temperature foods with one or two hot, pass-around appetisers. When deciding the menu, select foods that can be easily eaten in one or two bites and supplement with salty snacks such as olives or nuts. Hire a server or ask a friend to assist with passing the food around and replenishing drinks. To allow sufficient space for guests to circulate, group the food and drinks on high cocktail tables.

**Above:** Tape a sprig of mint to the top of a kebab stick. Thread the stick with seasonal fruit and place in a glass jug filled with water.

**Above:** Fold napkins into a rectangular shape, pile and tie together with a ribbon. Place on a tray topped with a flower and scatter pebbles on the side. This tray can be used for décor or serving purposes too.

**Above:** Print the menu on paper the size of the diameter of the base plate. Glue an edge of miniature rosebuds down the right-hand side of the menu. Place the menu inside a folded napkin, ensuring that the rosebuds are visible, then arrange on the plate.

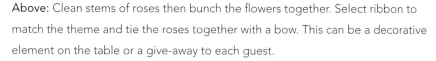

**Above:** Clean stems of roses then bunch the flowers together. Select ribbon to match the theme and tie the roses together with a bow. This can be a decorative element on the table or a give-away to each guest.

# Formal winter dinner

Break the cycle of cold nights and drab days by hosting a formal winter dinner. Light a fire in the fireplace just before the guests arrive and have extra logs on hand. Ask one of the guests to look after the fire throughout the evening. Bring warmth into the décor with yellow, orange and red flowers. Continue the theme of warmth when selecting the colour of the crockery and glassware. Use a variety of candles in different styles of candleholder and dim the lights to create a cozy atmosphere. Before plating the food, heat the crockery ahead of time in the warming drawer. Sumptuous food, opulent flowers, the flickering flames of a log fire reflecting off crystal glasses, and the companionship of good friends will certainly take the chill out of the winter season.

# Grilling party

A braai or grilling party is an easy and informal way of entertaining. The smoky aroma of outdoor cooking and the anticipation of delicious food sets the tone for a relaxed party. When planning the meal it should be easy to prepare, easy to eat and easy to clear away. Plan the menu so that the dishes don't all need to be cooked on the same fire at once. The African chic of this grilling party is created by the use of hanging lanterns and woven baskets set out in the bushveld. Use rugs, skins, chairs and pillows to create a seating area reminiscent of this scene. Bring elements of nature into the setting and combine an informal, relaxed occasion into a celebration of the outdoors.

**Above:** Cut a small slit into the bottom side of a decorative block of wood suitable in size to fit over the handle of the potjie lid. To hold it in place, drill a hole through the bottom section and insert a split pin.

**Above:** Arrange combinations of furniture, woven baskets and urns to create a lounge and dining area. Add décor elements such as sticks, ostrich eggs, monkey balls, pheasant feathers and pods. Use faux fur throws and cow hides to suit the natural surroundings.

**Right:** Fold the napkin in a rectangular shape that fits the size of the dinner plate. Place the napkin on the dinner plate and lay a colourful side plate on top of the napkin. Add additional colour with a smaller side plate of a different colour to enhance the place setting. Tie a metre of ribbon around the place setting and make a bow. Trim the edges of the ribbon accordingly. Cut some fresh flowers and berries and place into the ribbon as extra decoration. Lay the whole setting on an oval grass placemat.

# Picnic

Something exciting happens when entertaining outdoors. Food somehow tastes different in the open air and being outside among the natural elements creates a relaxing atmosphere that enables the picnic to flow freely. Outdoor entertaining can present a few logistical challenges such as keeping food hot or cold and coping with weather changes. Nevertheless, the décor touches will do half the work and the tranquil surroundings will do the rest! Bundling cutlery in a napkin makes transporting and serving easier and adds a decorative element to the picnic. Lay a bundle directly on the plate or, if serving buffet style, stand the bundles upright in a small basket. The picnic setting is created by layering throws and a multitude of soft scatter cushions, presenting an inviting seating area. The flowers in the basket of the bicycle add a whimsical touch, which is simple yet effective in creating the scene.

**Left:** Clean the stems of the flowers and shape into a bunch. Tie ribbon at the top of the stems and make a knot. Take the ribbon to the back of the bunch, crossover and twist either side to the front. Tie another knot and repeat to the end of the stems. End with a knot and a small bow.

# Pool party

Sparkling blue water provides the perfect backdrop for the bright colours of the décor used in the setting of this pool party. The unusual use of a glass table in the pool provides a captivating focal point. Combine different sets of cushions in a variety of colours with brightly coloured towels to tie in with the coloured glass vases as they reflect on the surface of the pool. A collection of coloured plastic containers placed around the pool complements the colours in the setting. Use bold flowers to add to the tropical feeling.

NB! In the interests of safety, if anyone is intending to swim, remember to use plastic glasses and crockery in the pool where possible.

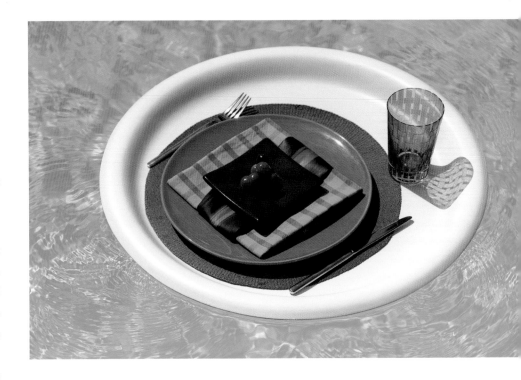

**Above:** Fold a napkin into a square and wrap a broad, green leaf (or a ribbon) around it. Place the napkin onto an underplate and position a side plate on top. Decorate the side plate with fresh chillies. Lay a place mat onto a white plastic tray and set with the prepared crockery, cutlery and a glass. Float the tray on water.

**Right:** Arrange different shapes of coloured vases on a glass table. Fill the vases with brightly coloured flowers. This can be used as a centrepiece.

# Tea party

A traditional tea party has timeless appeal and is an ideal choice for a daytime celebration. Arrangements of garden roses in harmonising colours create an inviting ambience. Silver trays and a tea service, classic crockery and linens add to the feeling of gracious elegance. Arrange comfortable chairs around a low table and serve the food on small plates that balance easily on guests' laps. Don't forget a variety of perfectly brewed teas.

**Above:** Fill a silver and glass cookie jar with assorted coloured rose petals. This can be used as a centrepiece or as a decorative element on the serving table.

**Above:** Using a glue gun, glue a ribbon around the crown of a hat and make a bow at the back. Remove stems from wide open roses and glue the roses and some of the leaves onto and around the brim of the hat.

**Right:** Fold a napkin into a rectangular shape (the size of the underplate) and place next to the underplate. Using a different colour napkin, fold it slightly smaller than the first napkin and place onto the first napkin. Set the cutlery on top.

# Retro party

Creating a special environment for a party is one of the most exciting things to do. It provides an opportunity to transport guests away from the everyday to a fantasy. The elements of the table do not have to be expensive, but to be memorable they must be original. To set the scene for this retro party the décor is kept minimal, with the focus on the striking crockery. The red from the crockery is used as a focal point and the use of the red vases, tea lights and tulips tie the theme together. Layering folded napkins and placing the cutlery on top creates a simple yet effective place setting that draws attention to the table. Unusual, quirky objects placed around the room further enhance the eclectic feel of this setting.

Left: Cut the flowers, leaving only a 5-cm stem, then bunch together. Find the centre of the napkin and position the flowers in the middle. Tie a ribbon around the napkin and the stems of the flowers. Arrange on the place setting and open the ends of the napkin to create a decorative design.

# Festive celebration

Polish the silver, take out your best crockery, set the table in the dining room and invite your family for an unforgettable celebration! Use linens and flowers in bold colours and position candles for accent lighting. Cloth napkins will complement the table setting. The candles should be either short or tall enough so that the flames are below or above the guests' heads. Small, matching arrangements of flowers can be placed around the room to create focal points and to tie the décor together. Use a mix of contemporary serving dishes and traditional or antique pieces. The floral balls in shades of purple in gold and black vases are highlighted by the use of candles and provide a spectacular focal point for this festive celebration. The striking tablecloth and matching napkins add a dramatic touch to the festivities.

# Buffet party

The scene for the buffet party is set in a forest where the angular shapes of the décor are in stark contrast to the natural surroundings. The idea of angular shapes contrasting with the natural is carried throughout the theme by potting orchids in square glass vases and placing pine cones in a glass dish. To bring this theme into the home, keep the setting simple and uncluttered. Arrange seating areas away from the buffet with plenty of space around the buffet for easy access. Set the serving platters on the buffet ahead of time and place the food at different heights to create an attractive look and for ease of serving. Set the plates at the starting point and the napkins and cutlery at the end so that the guests won't have to hold them whilst helping themselves to food. If the weather is cool, have shawls and throws on hand to keep the guests warm; these can be utilised in the décor during the early part of the party.

**Above:** Firmly squeeze and pull the stem of an Arum Lily from top to bottom until it softens and shapes into a circle. Place on a dinner plate.

# Midweek family dinner

This family dinner is made special and effortless by serving familiar food in a homely environment. The secret to making midweek entertaining work is a casual style of serving as well as an uncomplicated menu. The food is served family style from platters and bowls and there is nothing formal about the occasion. There is something appealing about the look of food served on blue and white crockery. Keep the look chic but low-key by incorporating masses of white flowers in blue and white containers. Continue the theme with blue and white candles, linen napkins and crockery. Using what is available around the home and including it into the setting creates a charming scene and is evocative of long lost traditions of family meals. Guests will appreciate the understated simplicity of this comforting setting and hearty meal.

**Right:** Tie bunches of cutlery together with ribbon and place onto stacked plates.

# Red, white and green party

This Italian-inspired menu is easy to prepare, and can be served in the kitchen or at the table *al fresco* style. Fresh seasonal ingredients and a little presentational style is all that is needed. The scene for the red, white and green party is set by the vegetable pyramid creating the focal point. Potted red flowers provide an accent of colour that is picked up throughout the theme by the coloured glassware and candleholder. Everyday crockery in colourful modern designs suits this menu perfectly. Terracotta pots and woven baskets add to the rustic feel of the occasion. Include a touch of nature with potted herbs and garden foliage, and create a sense of unity with uniformly folded napkins and coloured glasses. Keep store-bought items such as olives and marinated vegetables on hand to add to the *hors d'oeuvres*.

**Above:** Position a pedestal and place a 60 x 60 x 2 cm square wooden board on top. Cover the board with blocks of soaked oasis and create a pyramid using more soaked oasis. Secure the oasis blocks with kebab sticks. Skewer assorted vegetables onto kebab sticks and arrange into the oasis until it is completely covered.

**Right:** Wrap raffia around a freshly baked bread roll and tie a bow. Garnish with a sprig of fresh mixed herbs and place onto a side plate.

# Glossary

**Al dente** An Italian phrase meaning 'to the tooth', to describe pasta that is cooked until soft, but not over-cooked.

**Asian rice paper** An edible, translucent paper made from a dough of water and the inner stem of the rice paper tree.

**Bake** Cooking in the oven by means of dry heat. This method is used for cakes, biscuits, pastries and many other dishes.

**Bake blind** Baking a pastry case before filling it. The uncooked pastry is lined with baking paper and filled with dry beans or uncooked rice to stop it rising.

**Baking powder** Raising agent comprising two parts cream of tartar to one part bicarbonate of soda.

**Baste** Spooning the pan juices over meat or poultry during roasting, preventing it from drying out.

**Batter** An uncooked mixture of flour, liquid and a raising agent such as baking powder.

**Bicarbonate of soda** A component of baking powder. It acts as a raising agent when combined with cream of tartar.

**Blanche** Immersing fruit or vegetables in boiling water for a short period, and then in iced water.

**Blend** Mixing two or more ingredients together with a spoon or food mixer until combined.

**Blini** Small pancakes that are traditionally served with sour cream and caviar or smoked salmon.

**Boil** Cooking food in a boiling liquid.

**Bread flour** Also known as strong flour.

**Broth** A liquid resulting from cooking vegetables, meat or fish in water.

**Brown** Meat that is to be pot-roasted, stewed or casseroled should first be browned in hot oil or a dry, heavy-based pan. This seals the meat and prevents the loss of juices.

**Butter** The most commonly used fat for cake-making as it creams well and has the best flavour.

**Cake flour** Also known as plain flour.

**Casserole** A heatproof, deep baking dish with a tightly fitting lid used for cooking meat, poultry or vegetables.

**Chop** Cutting food into small pieces. Ingredients are chopped on a chopping board with a sharp knife in a quick up-and-down action. Food processors may also be used for this purpose.

**Coat** This term refers to covering food with an outer 'coating'.

**Cornflour** Fine white powder made from maize or wheat.

**Cream of tartar** The acid ingredient in baking powder.

**Cream together** Beating butter or sugar until light and creamy. Electric beaters or a rotary beater can be used.

**Croutons** Small cubes of fried or toasted bread that are usually served as an accompaniment or garnish to soup or salad.

**Dough** A thick, viscous mixture of flour and liquid.

**Dry-fry** The process of cooking food in a heavy-based saucepan or frying pan without using fat or cooking oil.

**Dust** Covering lightly with icing sugar or cocoa powder that is sifted over the top of a cake or tart prior to serving.

**Filleted** Removing bones from a piece of meat or fish, resulting in a fillet.

**Fold** Using a gentle motion to incorporate air into the mixture.

**Fry** The process of cooking food in a heavy-based saucepan or frying pan using fat or cooking oil.

**Garnish** An edible decoration such as parsley or lemon slices arranged around or on top of a savoury dish to improve its appearance and flavour.

**Gelatine** A colourless and tasteless setting agent. Six leaves are equivalent to 3 teaspoons of powdered gelatine.

**Glaze** A thin, glossy coating for both hot and cold foods.

**Granadilla** Also known as passionfruit.

**Grate** Shred by rubbing against a rough or sharply perforated surface.

**Grill** Cooking food by direct heat under a grill or over hot coals.

**Hard-crack stage** A test for sugar syrup; the point at which a drop of boiling syrup immersed in cold water separates into hard, brittle threads. Boil the sugar to 150–160 °C if using a sugar thermometer.

**Hull** Removing the leafy portion at the top of strawberries.

**Julienne** Cutting food into thin strips.

**Knead** Work dough by hand on a flat, floured surface. The dough is punched to develop the gluten in the flour.

**Marinade** A mixture of oil and vinegar, lemon juice or wine in which food is left to soak over a given time.

**Pastry** Dough made from a combination of flour, butter and liquid.

**Poach** Cooking food gently in liquid just below the boiling point.

**Potjiekos** Food that is slowly simmered in a cast-iron pot over an open charcoal fire.

**Prove** Last rising before the baking process and the shaping of the dough, and leaving it to rise on a baking sheet until doubled in size before baking.

**Punch down** Yeast dough is punched down after the first rising, shaped and left to rise for a second time.

**Purée** Food that has been liquidised in a food processor (fitted with a metal blade) until smooth.

**Red velvet** The combination of cocoa, baking powder and red food colouring in the presence of heat, resulting in the distinctive red colour.

**Rind** Outer layer of all citrus fruit.

**Roast** The process of cooking meat or poultry, uncovered, in the oven on the rack of a roasting pan without any additional fat or cooking oil.

**Rub in** Combining flour and butter or margarine with the fingertips until the mixture resembles bread crumbs.

**Sauté** Cooking food rapidly in a small amount of oil or other fat over direct heat.

**Searing** Rapidly browning meat in a little fat before grilling or roasting.

**Season** Flavouring foods in order to improve their taste.

**Self-raising flour** Cake flour sifted with baking powder in the proportion of 250 ml flour to 10 ml baking powder.

**Sift** Aerating a dry ingredient through a sieve to remove lumps.

**Simmer** Combining ingredients in a heavy-based saucepan with a lid and, once boiling, reducing the heat.

**Sterilise** Filling empty jars with boiling water for 10 minutes and draining.

**Sugar, caramel brown** Soft, fine granulated sugar containing molasses to give it its characteristic colour.

**Sugar, castor** Fine, granulated table sugar.

**Sugar, golden brown** Coarse, granulated yellow sugar.

**Sugar, icing** Confectioner's sugar.

**Sugar, white** Coarse, granulated table sugar.

**Syrup, golden** Thick sticky syrup with a deep golden colour.

**Thickening** Adding flour or cornflour to thicken soups, sauces or gravies.

**Tian** A shallow earthenware casserole containing layers of sliced vegetables. It is baked until tender.

**Truss** Securing poultry with string, pins or skewers to maintain a compact shape during cooking.

**Vanilla essence** Distilled from the seeds of the vanilla pod.

**Vanilla pod** Fruit of an orchid plant found in Madagascar, off the coast of Africa. The pod has a rich, sweet flavour.

**Verjuice** An acidic, slightly sour liquid made from unripe fruit – primarily grapes and sometimes apples.

**Whip** Beating ingredients such as egg whites or cream until light and fluffy.

**Whisk** Beating with a light, rapid movement using a whisk.

**Yeast, instant dry** Raising agent, which is packaged, and added to liquid or mixed directly into the dry ingredients.

# Index

# Conversion Chart

| METRIC | US CUPS | IMPERIAL |
|--------|---------|----------|
| 1 ml | ¼ tsp | – |
| 2–3 ml | ½ tsp | – |
| 4 ml | ¾ tsp | – |
| 5 ml | 1 tsp | ³⁄₁₆ fl oz |
| 15 ml | 1 Tbsp | ½ fl oz |
| 25 ml | | 1 fl oz |
| 50 ml | | 2 fl oz |
| 60 ml | 4 Tbsp | 2 fl oz |
| 80 ml | ⅓ cup | 2 ¾ fl oz |
| 125 ml | ½ cup | 4 fl oz |
| 200 ml | ¾ cup | 7 fl oz |
| 250 ml | 1 cup | 9 fl oz |
| | | |
| 25 g | – | 1 oz |
| 50 g | – | 2 oz |
| 75 g | – | 3 oz |
| 100 g | – | 4 oz |
| 150 g | – | 5 oz |
| 200 g | – | 7 oz |
| 250 g | – | 9 oz |
| 500 g | – | 1 lb 2 oz |
| 750 g | – | 1 lb 10 oz |
| 1 kg | – | 2 lb 4 oz |

# Oven Temperatures

| °C CELSIUS | °F FAHRENHEIT | GAS MARK |
|------------|---------------|----------|
| 100 °C | 200 °F | ¼ |
| 110 °C | 225 °F | ¼ |
| 120 °C | 250 °F | 1 |
| 140 °C | 275 °F | 1 |
| 150 °C | 300 °F | 2 |
| 160 °C | 325 °F | 3 |
| 180 °C | 350 °F | 4 |
| 190 °C | 375 °F | 5 |
| 200 °C | 400 °F | 6 |
| 220 °C | 425 °F | 7 |
| 230 °C | 450 °F | 8 |
| 240 °C | 475 °F | 9 |